Here's what educators, athletes & business leaders are saying:

"Timely & brilliantly written."

"An exquisitely timely and priceless lesson in life encapsulated in an engaging and valuable book. Brilliantly written and delightfully presented with a wonderful balance and sense of humor. "RICH WITHOUT MONEY" is a short and effective course in how to make each of our lives a great and more-fulfilling adventure. Laugh and learn as this great down-to-earth work captures you with its "real life" approach."

Dr. Frances Bartlett Kinne
Chancellor Emeritus and Past President
Jacksonville University
Jacksonville, FL

"Success occurs when preparation meets opportunity. This book can help you with both."

Nolan Ryan
#34
Banker, Rancher, Restaurateur
and Member, Major League Baseball Hall of Fame
Alvin, TX

"Richness comes from doing the things in life we are most passionate about. Leading teams of professionals to achieve significant goals is about being in touch with each person's unique skills and deepest desires. It is the combination of this diverse set of dreams that makes the attainment of something truly great possible. It is in the pursuit of that which has never been attained that inspires souls and changes lives. Winners understand that life's scoreboard will hold you accountable, not for what you have accumulated, but what you gave.

"I endorse "RICH WITHOUT MONEY." My Mom and Dad taught me early on that the richest moments in my life had everything to do with our love for one another and little to do with financial security. God, how I cherish those family vacations when my Dad spent every penny of his two-week paycheck, leaving only enough money to get the car back in the driveway for the ride home. I hope some day my sons can feel that way about what I gave them. If I attain this, I will have lived a great life."

William R. "Bill" McDermott
Executive VP of Worldwide Sales Operations
Siebel Systems, Inc.
San Mateo, CA

"A road map for achieving balance and contentment."

"RICH WITHOUT MONEY" is a wake-up call for all us in the fast lane of the 21st Century. By showing the reader how to tie their core values and passions into daily actions and activities, Simendinger provides a road map for achieving emotional balance and contentment in this journey called Life."

Marianne Nahin
VP Sales, ADVO, Inc.
Newport Beach, CA

"Pays huge and powerful dividends."

"If you have not been lucky enough to see Ted in action, this book is the next best thing. "RICH WITHOUT MONEY" is a quick read, but will pay huge and powerful dividends."

Mark W. Welle
Managing Director
Lexmark International Inc.
Denver, CO

"Read it, Do it, and Share it."

"RICH WITHOUT MONEY" is a book filled with many nuggets … practical and usable the next day. It is "*7 Habits*-like" but easier and more fun to read. "RICH WITHOUT MONEY" is a *"Read it, Do it, and Share it"* book that will make a difference."

Michael B. O'Neil, Ph.D.
President, The O'Neil Group Inc.
Building Leaders and Teams since 1975
Avon, CT

"For the heart, from the heart."

"Simendinger has done it again! A home run. A **must read** for anyone going to college, graduated from college or who knows someone who went to college. Ted, with his down-to-earth and common sense approach to living, gives us all a guide to live a better life. His tales of friendship, motivation, and core values make anyone who doesn't know him want to. For those of us who do know him, "RICH WITHOUT MONEY" brings together his philosophy of life in an enjoyable, well written, "how to" style.

"RICH WITHOUT MONEY" is a book written for the heart, from the heart."

Stephen Mayer
Founder, President & CEO
Burr, Pilger & Mayer CPA and the BPM Family of Firms
San Francisco, CA

"Enhances both your personal and business lives."

"RICH WITHOUT MONEY" is filled with actionable exercises to enhance both your personal and business lives. Ted has a passion for life that is evident in his anecdotes and the nuggets of knowledge he provides the reader. He is living his life on the Pro Leisure Tour (the PLT) and invites you to join him."

Dick Kievit
Vice President, retired, 33 years
Xerox Corporation
Pittsford, NY

"A powerful set of life improvement skills."

"This book has *"Success"* written all over it! The lighthearted, conver-sational style makes it very entertaining without losing its very serious message. The author's style engages the reader and drives home a powerful set of life improvement skills right from the very first page."

Linda O. Stewart
Vice President, Co-Counsel, Inc.
Fort Worth, TX

"Helps clarify goals & live a better life."

"RICH WITHOUT MONEY" uniquely combines real life stories with usable tools for enriching all aspects of your life. With humor and grace, Ted reminds us that how we think makes all the difference. His ideas will help anyone clarify their goals, live a better life, and enjoy the journey."

Chip Ford
Husband, Dad & Principal
Pineno & Levin Asset Management
Richmond, VA

"The best career advice I've ever found."

"I have worked in the recruiting and placement business for many years, and Ted's book offers the best career advice I've ever found. It will become the bible for our recruiters and career counselors."

Scott Dow
Co-Founder & CEO
Employmentlab
Dallas, TX

To Rod:
Thanks for your help &
support.
Best always,
12/01

RICH WITHOUT MONEY:

Life Skills

For

Better Business & Living

BY

TED SIMENDINGER

Airplane Reader Publishing
Denver, Colorado U. S. A.

First Edition

Book cover design by Karen Saunders, Denver, Colorado USA.

Library of Congress Cataloging-in-Publication Data

Simendinger, Ted.
    rich without money: life skills for better business & living / Ted
Simendinger. − 1st edition.

    ISBN 0-9702405-3-8

    1. Self Improvement.   2. Business.   3. Life Skills.   4. Title.

    Library of Congress Control Number: 2001119174

        10 9 8 7 6 5 4 3 2 1

    Published by Airplane Reader Publishing
            Denver, Colorado

Proudly printed in the United States of America

"Life is Good!"
A Dedication to George

The fellow who was supposed to make the final read of this manuscript never got to. He and his wife Diane were taken hostage on American Airlines Flight #77 and died on September 11, 2001 when their terrorist-commandeered plane was intentionally crashed into the Pentagon.

They died less than 20 miles from their home in Great Falls, Virginia. The pair was headed to Hawaii to fulfill her late father's dying wish to scatter his ashes on the islands he loved so much. They, of course, never made it.

I spoke with George the day before he died. He was proud to help with this book and I will be forever grateful he did. He, like me, believed it would help a lot of people.

For 30 years, George was the manager of training for Xerox Corporation – a rock-solid professional who knew as much about people, adult learning, personal growth and skills development as anyone I've ever known.

George had a very simple motto he repeated a million times during the 20 years I knew him. *"Life is good,"* he'd say with a giant cherubic grin. *"Life is good!"*

Each of us has two choices how we choose to live: We can take what life gives us or we can squeeze as much as possible out of each and every day.

George was a squeezer. And I sure will miss him.

George W. Simmons
Arrived: July 16, 1944
Departed: September 11, 2001

Special Thanks

The title for this book came out of a conversation during a phone call from Beijing, China to Auckland, New Zealand. A close friend, Lloyd Hill, lost his brother Dean unexpectedly and during the course of our talk, we both spoke about how much our friendships meant to each other – and how that if you live a life rich without money, you can avoid having material wealth become a yardstick of happiness.

This book was written for one simple reason: To help people. I wanted to give folks a reality-based guide that provided new ideas, helpful points of view and instantly usable skills. And I wanted those skills to be life skills – not just business or home skills – but valuable skills transferable to any circumstance.

I'm grateful for the sunshine and support of those who've helped bring this book to the shelf in the form I hoped for. They include Sherry Clawson and Nolan Ryan from Alvin, Texas; Fran Kinne from Jacksonville, Florida; Rich Cardillo from Evergreen, Colorado and my brother Mark from Edgewood, Kentucky.

I also need to think my omnipotent pal Luther – who seems to be everywhere all the time -- even though half that time I can't ever find him.

An extra special thanks to all the men and women who made the time to read the drafts and make this book as good as we, collaboratively, could make it. Those thanks extend to the book's cover illustrator, Karen Saunders. The kindness of folks willing to help others often know no boundaries, as all these fine people continually demonstrate.

Thanks too to my lovely wife Bonnie and my irrepressible pre-teen Gracie. It's easy to get up in the morning when you've got so much to live for.

And thanks to you, too, for reading. I hope you enjoy it.

Ted Simendinger

RICH WITHOUT MONEY
"Life Skills for Better Business & Living"

x

Section One:

THE

PAST

THE BRIDGE TO REALITY
(WHAT COLLEGE FORGOT TO TEACH!)

&

Rich Without Money

(What the world can teach us, too.)

Chapter 1

THE BRIDGE TO REALITY
WHAT COLLEGE FORGOT TO TEACH

It's a funny thing about growing up: We listen to everything our wise and perfect parents say until those wonderful teen years and then, late one Saturday morning, we wake up, straggle out of bed, and yawningly stretch and squint in the mirror. On this special day, we suddenly realize we know more than our folks about *everything* and choose to tune them out for a decade or two.

Just as surprisingly – a decade or two later – one morning we wake up and suddenly realize our parents aren't as dumb as they used to be. Somehow, some way, they suddenly got smart again.

At 17, I finished high school in Maryland and left home to attend college at a small private college near the ocean in Northeast Florida. Like a lot of kids, I moved away for a handful of reasons that were important to me at the time.

For example, I wanted to get far enough away from home I had to learn to solve my own problems. It was time to escape the shadow of my parents and not be able to run back home every time something inconvenient popped up. Leaving home was good for another reason, too – there would be far fewer witnesses when I messed up.

I also wanted to go to a small school where I was an individual student and not a social security number. Had I stuck around and gone to the University of Maryland, there would have been 235 students in my freshman biology class – hardly ideal for instructor interaction. I didn't want that. To this day, I much prefer small seminar groups when teaching or developing talent.

It's been my experience that interactive learning is light-years more effective than the stand-up method of lectern lecturing – especially when working with adults.

Lastly, I needed to work my way through college and still be able to pass. My folks had four kids and five extra dollars so I knew I had to pay my own way through school if I wanted to go. I wasn't a great student but went to class, tried hard, and graduated on time in eight semesters.

It was here I learned the value of two critical life skills: Hard work and time management. They remain among the most valuable of lessons I've ever learned and remain the guardian curbs of the paved road leading to life on the Pro Leisure Tour.

Life on the PLT means getting done in life what you want to – and need to – while carefully balancing other important wants and desires. Smart work in a straight line toward a clearly-understood goal is a powerful key to living a life rich in personal and professional fulfillment.

And that's what this book is about: *How to create, live and protect a fulfilling life balance with minimal wasted effort.*

Living Life on the Pro Leisure Tour is an attitude with both eyes locked onto a very reachable destination. This book is a how-to guide written to usher you along.

Years ago I arrived at college expecting four years of answers to bubble up out of a fountain of secrets and nourish me as I stepped aboard an escalator ride to the rich rewards of a Pro Leisure Lifestyle.

It sure didn't turn out that way. College really only teaches *some* (and not all) of the transitory things you need to learn in order to walk the gangplank of teenhood to an adult's version of reality. We all have to make that trip – from being a kid to becoming, at least in theory, a real live grown-up.

After all, finishing high school seems like a great concept until the instant that graduation mortarboard happily tossed high in celebration lands with a thud back on earth. Once that thing hits the ground, *that's* the moment when adulthood really begins.

Like most of my friends, I had no *clue* what to do after high school so I trundled off to college. I figured college bought me four more years to figure it all out.

A lot of kids who followed high school with college did so because, like me, they preferred wading into Lake Adulthood to boldly leaping right on in.

Most kids would rather not *have* to jump. They'd rather check the water temperature, the firmness of the lake bottom, and make sure they wore the right style swimsuit.

More importantly, many kids like the idea of being able to safely wade in and then scuttle right back out again whenever they want.

For some of those pals, entering college was nothing more than 13th grade – an extra year of high school, this one funded by their parents.

For others, ones who knew exactly what they wanted to study, college marked a new life chapter, especially true for those leaving home and traveling too far to drive back every time something unsettling happened. They eagerly awaited the cerebral challenges of a well-defined career path, personal growth and polish, and utilizing the surrounding resources of a great institution. College was a new and healthy type of forced responsibility. It wasn't always convenient but wasn't supposed to be. These folks gladly embraced the challenge such a valuable opportunity presented.

Some of my other friends were tired of school and had no interest in college whatsoever. They went to work immediately – they just sort of dived into Lake Adulthood and started swimming. They didn't care how cold or deep the water was since they knew they could change neither and realized they'd have to get wet sooner or later.

They chose sooner. *Splash!* In they dove and off they went. Some were good swimmers. Others dog-paddled. Some still do.

I was a chicken. I preferred wading to diving so I went away to school and bought myself more time.

Some friends *weren't* perplexed by the future, knew *exactly* where they wanted to attend school, what they wanted to learn, and what they wanted to do for a living once they finished.

I had a totally different problem: I didn't have a foggy clue what to study. "Rudderless" would seem to be the perfect glove-fitting adjective. "Puzzled" and "bewildered" also come to mind.

I enrolled in general studies. Once I arrived, there were really only two things I wanted to get *out* of college. One was a diploma. I had heard they were important but had no clue why. I perceived a diploma as necessary – sort of like a subway token to the future. As I understood it, college would teach me everything I had to know to become a rich sophisticated adult and the diploma was my passport – the scroll of proof that I was fully-qualified and well-deserving of having the finer things in life handed to me.

The second thing I wanted was to emerge able to land a job that enabled me to earn enough money to buy my own house. My castle need not be big or fancy fortress or even have a moat. It simply needed to be mine. It would be extra-nice if the keys to the house were handed over along with my diploma, but I wasn't exactly certain how all those things tied together.

But there was a lot of living – and a lot of learning – between the day I showed up for school and the day I left. And truth be told, as the college experience evolved, I did, in fact, begin learning a few things.

Like a lot of kids, I worked full-time while grinding my way through school. I had a good job – a meat-cutter in a grocery store – so I literally *was* grinding my way through school. I learned a trade, made good money, worked hard, and sliced myself to O-positive blood-leaking ribbons day-after-bloody-day for four straight years.

I bled more than the meat did. To this very day, you can still play tic-tac-toe among the self-inflicted scars of my fingers.

College life wasn't exciting like it was supposed to be. Class from 8-to-1, then work from 1:30-to-9:30. I bled the most from about 3-to-5:30. Bandaged up for mealtime.

After work, I studied from 10-to-midnight. Got up and did it all again the next day. That was life for four straight years. Even the simplest of things I took for granted back home suddenly seemed harder than moonwalking to Paris.

Saving money seemed impossible. And it was sobering to learn that toilet paper no longer grew out of the wall and had to be purchased with take-home pay. Paying cash for *everything* was a concept with which I was totally unfamiliar.

It wasn't much of a life but it was all I had and between school and work I learned a lot. I almost had to, since I knew virtually nothing about anything the first day I showed up for each.

As an impoverished freshman, I learned that if you squeeze the tube hard enough, you'll never run out of toothpaste. Plus I learned that all major food groups could be purchased at 7-11. To this very day, the *"-os"* – Doritos, Cheetos, and Fritos – still fuel the nation's colleges. Pizza and Doritos fuel the furnaces of our future leaders.

I also quickly discovered that when it came to learning retention, you were much better off studying *before* having a beer than vice-versa. When I was a sophomore, I counseled several incoming freshmen about this important tidbit of wisdom. I was a mentor of sorts without even realizing it.

I'd entered college expecting to emerge fully educated in all relevant and necessary ways of the world. Some of my high school pals were really smart and scattered around attending much better schools than me – some of the nation's best. They even proved they were smarter than I was by taking out a college loan rather than working and bleeding-as-they-went.

Despite that, we *all* seemed to be learning many of the same important things – things like:

♦ If you visit a bar during "sink-or-swim night," you will sink.

- It wasn't a felony to wear different colored socks, but they sure made it harder to get a date.

- And that *"HIGH"* was the stovetop temperature by which all men cooked everything.

Bacon, eggs, burgers – you name it, we ignited it.   There wasn't a guy I knew who could cook *anything* you didn't have to eat in the dark.   We all cranked the stovetop dial and donned the sunglasses.   Cooking on *HIGH* required a young man's quickness. By my junior year I even learned that when you tested the doneness of spaghetti noodles by tossing them against the wall, you weren't supposed to leave them stuck to dry out on the tile.

By the time graduation rolled around, I had learned how to cut up a chicken in 24 seconds.   Incidentally, that number – 24 – is *exactly* the same number of self-scarred stitches I received en route to my diploma.   The night before graduation, I calculated I had cut 13,000 T-bone steaks and 250,000 pork chops as an undergrad.   I also remember thinking: *"That's enough, man, that's _enough_!* Hand me my diploma, the keys to my house, my closet full of clothes, surprise me with a car – I am *done!"*

But for a college job, meatcutting was a great trade to learn.   It paid well, I learned how animals fit together, it saved me during freshman biology and, by my senior year, I'd even learned to cook hot dogs on *"MEDIUM."*

But I looked forward to leaving college with fading memories and permanent scars.   Like my friends, I wanted to attack the real world as soon as possible.   It was time to don the swim trunks and jackknife gracefully into Lake Adulthood.

But the night before graduation I remember sitting on the edge of the bed in my apartment, staring at the Band-Aids encircling my index fingers.   I was more scared than happy.

Diploma or no diploma, I *hadn't* learned everything I needed to know and knew it.

No More School

In a flash, college was over. So, too, was force-fed book learning. My fellow graduates and I were jettisoned in individual space pods out into the real world, where new lessons from Reality University were force-fed and crammed down our throats whether we liked the taste or not.

So, while college often graded in a bell curve, the real world didn't. My friends and I immediately noticed the exact same thing: You had to produce, adjust, adapt, and improvise. You also had to learn to compete.

Like it or not, you *must* to be willing to compete. The competition started *immediately* for just about everything whether you liked it or not: You had to interview for jobs, fight for raises and promotions, and simultaneously deal with the heartbreak and emotional squirreling stemming from rejections and failed relationships.

It was a symphony of confusion out there but the calendar wouldn't wait. Things changed quickly. Very, very quickly.

For most, a working career began. Often, it took the form of a job rather than the zealous pursuit of a passion. The lucky women and men who entered college with a game plan and graduated with that plan well-executed were far ahead of the rest of us. They were following their passion.

The rest of us, meanwhile, just took jobs. There was a massive difference between chasing a passion and taking a job – a meaningful difference college somehow forgot to teach.

In the short run, simply taking a job might not matter. After all, it pays the bills. But in the long run, it always does. College prepares us to get a job. It does not teach us a *thing* about passion. Emptiness in life comes from a lack of passion. You need it. You absolutely need it. You need it in your personal life and you need it in your business life. People without passion stare out of a lot more windows than people with it. People with it are much too busy to waste the time.

Once out of school, a decent job means money. Financially, for the first time, more money might be coming in than going out. Some handle that well – paying themselves first, as they should. Others learn the hard way that college grads are easy pickings for multiple credit cards leading to quick debt accumulation.

A few years back at a high school reunion one of my pals told me that he spent his 30s paying for his 20s. I understood exactly what he meant. Debt was like trouble – far easier to get into than out of.

As the college years fade to distant memories, physical changes take place, too. The ride on mortality's emotional rollercoaster begins its lifelong sojourn from the energetic exuberance of a young person's present to the invisible twists and turns of hidden horizons. Babies joyfully arrive, parents and elderly loved ones tearfully depart. Old friends are found; dear friends are lost.

Rarely does any of it seem fair. Mortality is often inconvenient.

None of this is taught in college. For all of us, these are force-fed lessons learned far too early and concern things we never wanted to learn anyway. Like Robin Williams said, *"Whoa! Reality – what a concept!"*

For each of us, these new life challenges are steadily delivered one after another like hurrying travelers whisking up an airport escalator: Job, wedding, spouse, kid, house, dog, debt and payment books. They arrive one right after the next, like row after row of marching British Tories during the Revolutionary War. College doesn't prepare us for these things. Perhaps it should. Perhaps it couldn't.

With all these rapid changes thrust upon us, it's no wonder that from time-to-time we can all benefit from advice and steerage. When you look back at what college *really* teaches us, it's really about gaining enough book-knowledge to create a marketable skill set, coupled with the slowly-dawning awareness that life on the street is a lot more complicated than bunking in a dormitory.

For many, as families start, learning stops. There's no scorecard kept of what you learn once you quit sitting in uncomfortable chairs splitting time between staring at the chalkboard, glancing at classmates you daydreamed of dating and gazing out the window.

Some pursue learning outside the classroom, some don't. Some choose to grow and change – with new hobbies and interests – and some don't.

The need for learning is an internalized thing. Some people feed the need daily; others store it in their cerebral garage like an old pool table under a dusty canvas cover.

But college *doesn't* teach us the things we really need to learn to maximize not just what we do in life, but how we do it. It doesn't teach us motivation, leadership, communication, sales and persuasion, inspiration, or how to deal with change.

Nor does it even teach us where to go get a booster shot (much less a steady diet) of good old-fashioned common sense. The street seems to teach common sense a lot better than schools ever do, regardless the cost of tuition.

Think of those important life skills as its own growing branch on your personal tree. From each branch will stem *other* skills and traits. In the end, you'll have nurtured a strong, magnificent shade canopy for others to enjoy.

Individually, and collectively, these half-dozen skills are all *very* important things to learn, regardless how that learning comes about:

Motivation. Without motivation, we'll never achieve in life even *half* of what we potentially could. Even worse, we can't help others achieve half of what *they're* capable of, either.

Leadership. Without leadership, you'll never be as good a parent, friend, or neighbor as you could be. Like the sign on

George Steinbrenner's desk says, there are times to lead, times to follow, and times to get the heck out of the way.

Communication. Without the ability to communicate effectively, you'll never bring the joy, happiness and interpersonal effectiveness to your life and the lives of others that you're capable of demonstrating.

Selling. Everyone sells all the time – knowingly or unknowingly. Not products necessarily, but ideas and opinions and points-of-view.

Selling and persuasion are crafts that lean heavily on communication skills to succeed. It's what you say and how you say it that matters.

An old friend of mine, Emmett Reagan, used to use this example: "Ever tell someone they look twice as good today as yesterday?" he'd ask. "They light up, don't they? Men do, women do, everybody does. It's flattering. It's a compliment.

"Then," Emmett continued, "the *next* time you see them, tell them they ain't half as ugly as they used to be!

"And then *duck*," he added quickly with a laugh. "You're saying basically the same thing each time but the message is received totally differently.

"What you say or *mean to say* is one thing," he said. "But *how you say it* and *how it's received* are what matters most."

Inspiration & Passion. Inspiration is linked to passion like a kite to a string. People of passion are inspired. Inspiring people are porch lights that attract other people. Best of all, passion can mushroom from any facet of your life. We'll demonstrate the huge role passion plays in living a quality life in a later chapter.

For now, understand you _need_ passion in your life. Consider it necessary fuel – like air or water or food. Recognizing the need for passion is important. Deciding to chase it is a life choice.

Having passion in your life is very controllable. A lucky few learn its importance at home, in school, from a role model or soon after they begin working.

Most of us take longer to finally figure it out.

Dealing with Change. Change can be both the worst *and* the best part of living. Things change all the time. Some folks handle transition with ease. Others worry themselves to pieces and find change very uncomfortable.

We *can* manage worry and we *can* manage change. Embrace change for what it is – a new set of challenges and opportunities. Change is good. It helps you grow. Change might be inconvenient from time-to-time, but make no mistake – it *always* helps you grow.

Frustratingly, once our formal schooling ends – at whatever level that may be – all these vitally important life skills are things we need to learn and develop on our own.

Fortunately, we can. And it's really pretty easy.

After the Diploma:
What College *Forgot* to Teach

Like many, I graduated college with a business degree. I studied business because that's what I thought the son of a businessman was supposed to do.

As I clutched the diploma handed over by William Simon, then-Secretary of the Treasury, I knew full-well college hadn't taught me everything I needed to know.

Ribbon-tied scroll safely in-hand, I immediately decided to parlay my business studies by moving back home to Annapolis to become a famous sportswriter. Great way to leverage four years of business education, wasn't it?

Thanks to my college accounting courses, when I got my first check from the newspaper I was able to sit down and figure out I'd taken a pay cut from my college job as a meatcutter. I traded the blood and guts of a refrigerated cutting room floor for the blood and guts of eking out a living in an air-conditioned emulation of *The Odd Couple's* Oscar Madison.

So, after a couple years of being a famous sportswriter, I opted for eating over not eating and decided to move back to Florida and get a real job. This is a common byproduct of the newspaper industry: Fun job, ego job, no cash job.

Needing to scrape together enough money to move, I quit the paper and opted for a quicker way to make some dough.

I trapped animals, mostly raccoons and muskrats. Much to their dismay, I was pretty good at it. I took the furs to Angler's Sporting Goods on Route 50 outside Annapolis and not far from the Chesapeake Bay Bridge.

I sold the pelts for cash on the spot and got enough to rent a little U-Haul trailer and finance my move from Maryland back to Florida.

I was pretty proud of myself until I blew a tire in South Carolina. I bought one for $35 that didn't fit the car, and eventually wobbled into Jacksonville determined to do two things.

One was work for someone who was the best in the world at what they did – which I ended up doing – and the other was marry my college sweetheart, who I had moved out on in the middle of the night when I sneaked out of town two years before. Unfortunately for me, she had a pretty good memory and things never quite worked out.

While interviewing for a real job, I soon ran out of fur money and found part-time work as a freelancer for the Florida Times-Union newspaper. My job was to type up the dog entries, race results, and all the stuff in tiny type that hardly anyone reads.

The paper only needed me three nights a week and I spent most of my days trying to locate something more permanent and better paying. I rarely spent more than $1 a day on food and bounced around at night from sofas to cots to friends' guest rooms.

14

To kill time late at night, since I had no money, I ran. Ran for miles, and hours. I knew that being physically fit would be a lifesaving offset for being fiscally destitute. Typically I ran through modest communities and dreamed of someday owning my own tiny home, just like the ones I passed every 125-feet. But my late night runs always took me *by* the homes, never *toward* them. Night after night they all remained teasingly beyond reality's reach.

For a guy with no cash and a fog-shrouded future, I sure did learn a lot. Here again it was a much different type of learning than college. Much of what I learned was learned in silence. And, like most stark reality lessons, they reshaped my values, personality and ambitions. When times are tough, the things you learn always seem to stick with you a lot deeper and longer than when times are good.

College teaches us a lot but we forget a lot, too. For example, I remember that Pi is 3.1416. But I've forgotten and have no foggy clue why I would ever need it for anything, unless I was on *"Who Wants to Be a Millionaire?"* and Regis asked me: "What number is six-tenths of a point higher than your college G.P.A.?"

Luckily for me, I soon caught a break and was hired by Xerox. Back then, they were about as good as an American company could be. Xerox plowed millions into attracting talent, developing it, polishing it to the highest professional standards and – most importantly – retaining it. They invested heavily in people and were truly the very best in the world at what they did. Suddenly the sun had risen brilliantly on life's dawning horizon.

Great companies aren't great companies by accident. I was immediately force-fed business knowledge, tactics, strategies and professionalism that college classes never mentioned. And, as the scope and perspective of day-to-day living changed, I quickly learned a lot of *other* things that college failed to cover.

Some were learned from business, some from the street, some from moving, some from travel, some from my friends and some from the simple osmosis of aging. None were the same things they'd taught me in school.

College forgot, for example, to teach that:

♦ *Good shoes are worth the money.* So, for that matter, is a good haircut. If you think a *bad* haircut looks bad the day you get it – just wait a couple days.

♦ *New York is for baseball caps and L.A. is for sunglasses.* There's a whole lot of USA separating these two cities – geographically, stylistically, and attitudinally. People are people – but people are all different and you must respect and embrace those differences. You can't be geographically judgmental.

♦ *Life's what you do between shaves.* And you can't live it on a sofa. Like Ted Turner said at a Notre Dame commencement address: *"You don't have to know anything to make something happen."*

♦ *Time marches on.* Time waits for no man. Or woman. The only way to stop it is to have a really bad hangover.

♦ *In a disagreement, someone doesn't always need to be right – or wrong, for that matter.* I learned that from my best friend the hard way, while my irascible father was dying of cancer. And my pal was right, as best friends often are. Differences don't always require a jury verdict of correctness.

♦ And, thanks to the bountiful dollars of working for Xerox but no thanks to the pinched pennies of the newspaper business, I learned that *a really great restaurant can dramatically accelerate the courtship ritual.*

A Dozen Things College *OUGHT* to Teach

Now, having said all that, here are 12 things more important than how to tap a keg that college *ought* to teach.

1. **Balance in life is just as important than money. Maybe even moreso.**

16

You will be happiest in life if you live a life where you're rich without money and don't measure your success by your possessions or portfolios. Money is good, however. You can't help the poor by becoming one of them.

2. *Being nice matters.*

The nicest man I ever met is one of the planet's most famous – Muhammad Ali. Muhammad lives a great Pro Leisure Tour life, on his terms. There's more about Ali in a later chapter and how he does it – and why I think he's one of the kindest men you'll ever meet.

Being nice was a learned skill for me. I did not have the best of relationships with my father and I grew up with a bit of a resentful chip on my shoulder. Ali's longtime trainer Angelo Dundee sat me down one day and explained why being nice mattered.

"Being nice to people makes you feel better about yourself," Angelo said. "Muhammad treats everyone like a king," he continued, "and that's one of the reasons everyone treats him like one, too."

Odd thing to hear from a fight trainer, isn't it? But Angie was right and I'm a better man for following his counsel. Kindness is contagious and it *does* fuel your own self-esteem. Being nice is also a mandatory behavior for living a life on the Pro Leisure Tour.

3. *You're never too old to seek role models, or too young to be one.*

If you're smart, you'll seek out role models for every major facet of your life – personal *and* professional. When you see an admirable trait, incorporate it. When you have a skill to help another, share it. Volunteer it, proactively.

4. *There's no such thing as "Can't Because."*

The words "can't because" are buzzwords from a loser's mentality. Instead, always ask, *"How can we?"*

Years ago, I struck the words "can't because" out of my personal lexicon. I've got rabbit ears for them and now when I hear "can't because" my teeth grate, nostrils flare, and I blink at least twice.

Whenever I hear "can't because" I search the eyes of the speaker and silently think, "Why not?" and wonder if, in fact, *they* might be part of the problem since *"Can't Becausers"* often are.

When you eliminate the words "can't because" from your personal dictionary and vote instead to look at challenges with those three words, you'll brainstorm new ideas. From those ideas will spring innovative solutions.

Do yourself a favor and embrace these three powerful little one-syllable words that use just eight little letters. Become a *"How can we?"* person. The sooner, the better.

Spread the message to others, too. Help rid the planet of *"Can't Becausers."* Be positive, not negative, and vocally lead by example. Urge others to embrace a *"How can we?"* type of thought approach to everything. Winners *always* think that way.

5. *No Stinkin' Thinkin.'*

Stinkin' thinkin' is another part of the loser's mentality. George Simmons, Xerox's long-time sales training manager at its world training center, coined this as his personal motto. A poster child for George's mantra is the most positive-thinking fellow you'll ever make the time to watch at work – golfing great Tiger Woods.

Tiger had a sports psychologist at the age of 10. If this golf thing doesn't work out for Tiger, he'd make one heck of great instructor himself. He expects success and wastes no energy on negative thought. Tiger envisions success and trusts his preparation to calmly deliver the results he expects.

6. *Focus on dignity of thought and expression.*

Speak to be understood and demand clarity of thought from others. Don't tolerate the nonsensical doublespeak so common in business.

Orlando healthcare executive Brian Crawford believes that corporate America is driving common sense and logic right out of

18

American industry. "Somebody needs to invent CSU," he told me one day in frustration. "Common Sense University. Nobody teaches it any more. Corporations get so tripped up in the CYA (protecting your posterior) mentality that too many people are losing every shred of common sense they ever had."

Avoid a sound bite existence. Think through issues carefully and communicate those views precisely.

And if you curse, curse less. There are nearly a half-million words in the English language. Too often you hear people rely on the seven most offensive.

7. Given a choice between moderation and fanaticism, go with moderation.

Anything done to extremes usually sacrifices balance. In the short run, it's OK to be overtly consumed by something. In the long run, it's not.

People with balance in life rarely fall off the balance beam of happiness. People *without* balance often wobble, then topple. Inner peace, happiness, and balanced life-fulfillment are key ingredients to a Pro Leisure Tour contentment.

Get too far out of whack what happens? Frustration, anger, fatigue, stress and negative thinking start entering the picture. For the long haul, stay balanced.

8. Technology creates tools of convenience, not gadgets to hide behind.

Technology can also create social ostracism and a lack of fitness, both physical *and* cerebral. Let the greatness of technology's tools provide more time, not less, to complement human interactions in life. Don't hide behind technology. Emerge and stay physically fit. Fitness makes everything easier. It staves off aging, too.

9. The harder you work at something you enjoy, the faster the clock's minute hand circles.

When you do things you love, a wristwatch is basically useless.

10. *Disagreements or differing points of view are sometimes simply a difference in perspective.*

Always seek to understand a differing perspective. Two quick family stories illustrate the point. One deals with a hatchet, the other a pigeon.

The Hatchet

My father was a bit of a troublemaker growing up and wasn't overly nice to anyone, including his younger brother.

One day my uncle got so tired of being belittled he finally snapped. He picked up a hatchet off the ground and angrily threw it toward my father after my father turned and walked away. To my uncle's horror, the hatchet thudded into the back of my father's skull.

My dad was OK, but had a lifetime scar to show for it. My uncle was terrified. A thousand negative thoughts instantly flooded his mind – one of which was he'd nearly killed his brother.

After getting whacked, my father stopped in his tracks, pivoted back around to face my uncle and said, simply, "Nice shot."

My father was proud his younger brother had finally – after a lifetime of being belittled and bullied – stood up and fought back.

The Pigeon

The second example involves my mother, who once spent all afternoon in a Philadelphia beauty parlor getting her hair done for a rare night out. Around 4 p.m. she finally emerged, hair coifed perfectly. My mom walked down the sidewalk toward the street and under a giant maple tree. The maple provided shade and a roost for some city pigeons. A pigeon dropped a bomb on top of my mother's new hairdo, which caused her to break out into parallel rivers of tears as she ran back inside the salon.

From *her* perspective, all her time and money had been wasted.

From the bird's perspective, it was one heck of a shot.

Remember: In a difference of opinion, someone need not always be right or wrong.   Respect the existence of differing perspectives.

11. *To a large extent, money is overrated.*

Time and money are both important but, between the two, *time* matters most.   Live within your means of both.

Money-wise, that means being fiscally responsible within the time/revenue balance created by the life that makes you happiest.

Time-wise, living within your means requires not overcommitting.

Whatever you choose to do, do well.   But respect and protect the pillared cornerstones of the house that keeps your life in balance.

I meet and work with a lot of people who've been sucked deep into the vortex of a sound-bite existence.   The more they try to do the less they seem to get done.   Treat your time like gold currency and zealously protect it from time robbers and embezzlers.

Juggling your time to get done what you need to in a quality way requires a blended balance of thoughtful strategizing with action-based decision-making.

A friend of mine died a few years back without ever having really lived.   All he ever did was feverishly work delivering newspapers or overseeing their delivery.   From the time he finished high school until he was buried at 35, he worked 12-to-16 hours a day, six or seven days a week.   It was an exhausting job he performed, not a self-fueled passion he pursued.

My pal was always working too hard, too often, to go find another line of work he'd enjoy a lot more.   He was overwhelmed by the merry-go-round lifestyle he was frantically whirling clockwise around.   He was always too busy to free up more spare time to be with his family and chase his hobbies.

His life ended two months after the headaches began and less than one month after his diagnosis. If life gave him a "do-over," my guess is he'd live more and work less. He also wouldn't die with cobwebs latticeworked to his beloved and woefully under-utilized fishing rods.

Don't wait until you bury a friend to learn such a valuable lesson.

12. *And lastly, college ought to teach us that part of our personal time management plans MUST include plenty of private time and rest.*

Life on the Pro Leisure Tour requires a comfortable balance of leisure, stress management, personal fulfillment and relaxation – all of which spoke back to a central need for enough regular rest to do your best at whatever you choose to do.

Prioritization, organization and efficient execution of day-to-day activities can enable anyone to move the relative mountains in his or her life. Rest is a necessary part of it. Know yourself well enough to have a plan for stress relief and quality relaxation.

College doesn't teach these things. But it should and maybe it would . . . *if pep rallies and frat parties weren't so darn important!*

Chapter 2

Rich Without Money

What Old Shoes & A Beat-up Suitcase Can Teach You

The true size of the planet is simply a matter of perspective. On one hand, it's a big world – but all you need to shrink it are comfortable shoes and a piece of old luggage.

Frizzy-haired Boston comedian Steven Wright has a different point of view. "It's a small world," he says in his trademarked deadpan monotone, "But I'd hate to have to paint it."

I have been very fortunate to travel the world playing a sport I love to play – baseball. Every country we've spent time in has taught us an enormous amount. Each trip helps shrinks the planet, too. It's almost like putting a belt around the equator and tugging it one notch tighter every time we go somewhere new.

I've popped out, grounded out and struck out looking in some amazing places: Cuba, Russia, Ukraine and China among them. We saw the still-warm byproduct of a Mafia hit at a hotel in Moscow; got pulled over at machine-gun-point on an empty road in Ukraine; witnessed the cultural tug-of-war of old China versus new; and found perhaps the nicest, kindest people in the world blanketed under the suffocating economic circumstances of Castro's Cuba.

Just 90 miles from Key West – closer than Palm Beach – the Cuban families we met were issued one small bar of soap a month. A crowded city block of people shared the use of a single telephone. Only government buildings were freshly-painted. Our e-mails home were intercepted, read, edited, and changed.

Horsemeat (much less beef) was a clandestine delicacy to most, since many people were tired of a redundant life eating only pork and chicken. The average worker earns about $20 per month.

23

Water trucks manually deliver small amounts of fresh water to many homes in Old Havana.

And yet, as destitute and impoverished as nearly all the Cuban citizenry are, they might very well be the nicest we've ever met anywhere in our travels. In many ways, despite terribly difficult times, they live their lives rich without money.

Cuba has none of the financial rocket-fuel being poured into its economy that China does. Cuba's a society withering brown on the ground like a dying vine in a Texas drought.

China is the opposite – an enormous nation wrestling with an incredibly accelerated pace of change. Anyone who keeps his or her ears and eyes open and mouth closed will be forever changed by a visit.

To frame the enormity of Beijing, the cities of New York and Los Angeles – added together – have about as many people as Beijing by itself. Further south, 20% of the world's entire fleet of supercranes are in Shanghai, filling the clouds with remarkable skyscrapers day after day after day.

In China, people work very hard, and very long, just to live. Outside the city, hundreds of millions of rural Chinese are destitute, impoverished peasants. Little is mechanized and there are few creature comforts. Consequently, they are a very fit and hard-working society. The only fat people in China are tourists.

The history of *our* nation goes back a couple hundred years. Theirs goes back *thousands*. The sheer age of the traditional Chinese culture, combined with the logistical scope of such a vast billion person society, highlights *why* fundamental change is so difficult.

So much of what we take for granted – personal space, for example, or transportation, or running hot water – are vividly contrasted to the lifestyles of the globe's most-populous country. There's no such thing as personal space in urban China. Family units will domicile in two-room homes 200 or 300-square-feet in size.

Like Russia, but for totally different reasons, China was such an eye-opener I went back a second time as soon as I had a chance.

Through it all, the good *and* bad, what I've learned is:

The world's worth seeing. The more you see, the more you learn and better you understand what the talking heads on TV are barking about.

You'll learn the most if you go where you don't speak the language. You'll *really* accelerate those learnings if you visit those places by yourself. Even better, pursue a hobby or interest while you travel because many of the foreigners you meet will share your same passion.

Reserve judgment on things beyond the boundaries of your experience. My views on Cuba, China and Russia, and the people who live there, have been exponentially enhanced by what I've witnessed. Always trust yourself more than any form of global media. The media interprets what they see and expresses things their own way. *You* interpret things *your* way.

Being different is good, not bad. Different cultures are good, different points of view are good. Foreign perspectives on U.S. news and news events are often totally different than our own. Right or wrong, better or worse, how the world sees us is not always the way we hope to be seen. In fact, it rarely is.

And, lastly, if you've seen <u>one</u> castle – well, quite frankly, you've seen them all. Castles are boring, unless it's your own.

A diverse work force is the gas pedal to the accelerator of economic change and social improvement. I'm not a big fan of quotas and percentages. I'm a fan of talent. And having taught skill development to thousands of professional marketeers over the years, I quickly realized that talent is colorblind, gender-blind, height-blind, and weight-blind.

Other factors matter more. Regardless of your background, which you can't change, if you've got the "want to," you're halfway home and you will achieve more in life than people who don't.

That's what the balance of this book is about: *Teaching those with the "want to" how to apply those desires to quickly and efficiently do more in life and business.*

The Power of Differentiation

According to the dictionary, "differentiation" means *"To make unlike; develop specialized differences in."*

Why is it important? Why does it matter? There are a *lot* of reasons. Travel the world and you'll quickly and dramatically witness the differentiation principle woven throughout the planet's spectacular mosaic of business and living. For example:

In Business: In businesses around the world, some people are motivated and some aren't. Some are optimistic and some aren't. Some have drive and ambition, some don't. Some are people who *make* things happen; some simply *watch* things happen. A few, of course, simply to sit like tree stumps behind desks and *wonder* what happened.

With Products: Products that are perceived interchangeable with others are considered to be commodities. Commodities are sold on price, since all features and capabilities are perceived to be the same. In commodity sales, the cheapest wins, the others lose. Products become more valuable if they are NOT the same as those of someone else. Every product should – whenever possible – *always* be differentiated. Creating differentiation in the perception of the customer is what the ad industry is all about.

For a quick moment, think about the different impressions your mind might generate by a seeing a label reading *"Made in USA"* versus another reading *"Made in China."*

Does something as simple as a label serve to differentiate things that might not otherwise be perceived differently?

How do *you* react to that simple difference in labels?

Between Companies: In free market economies, companies are really nothing but a herd of people making things happen that stockholders think is never quite good enough. Companies are the sum-total of the contributions of all its people, where pooled skills and efforts determine success.

That's why companies recruit, nurture, develop, and hope to retain talent since it's smarter and cheaper to keep good people than go find and train some more. The company harvests the results of the collaborative efforts and investments made in those people.

Companies, then, are differentiated not just by *what* they do but also by *how* they operate and the people they employ. Most advertise and sell those differences by brand name identification and reputation.

Among People: People everywhere are different on the outside, yet internally very much the same. If you leave the politics to the politicians and simply focus on the human aspects of the people you meet and friends you make, then Mark Twain was right: "People are all alike, on the inside."

Thank goodness we are! If we weren't, how confusing it would be to pick up our kids from school at the end of the day? It's *good* that people look, act, and sound differently.

Diversity has powerfully exciting potential for the 21st century. It's maddening sometimes, but always worth respecting and always well worth the proper investment in time, patience, and learned understanding.

People around the planet are inherently good, too. That holds true for the rich and poor, the intellects and unsophisticated, and from every country and continent.

During a keynote address in San Francisco, I said the three biggest reasons for America's recent economic boom were (in order):

1. *The embracement and integration of cultural diversity into the modern work force.* Smart work teams have learned to park egos and work collaboratively;

2. *The accelerated emergence and integration of new digital-based technologies into all aspects of production:* Front office, back office, manufacturing, distribution, etc.

3. *Corporations placing their customers first, and trusting the long-term health and viability of their organizations to fulfilling the wants, needs, and loyalties of a partnership-oriented client base.* Win/win relationships that strengthen over time will outlast revolving-door customer bases every single time. In business (and in life), strategic partnerships and caring friendships will last over time – while tactical ones *don't.*

Even now, as the American economic pendulum swings back the other way and global economies correct, the adaptive actions necessary to succeed will come from the pooled resources of all full-spectrumed points of view.

That, too, is another beauty of diversity: It accelerates success *quickly* in times of prosperity, and cross-pollinates solution ideas when times toughen. There is no downside to multicultural contributions of ideas and points of view.

Not everyone, of course, is a prosperous businessperson. To better frame the realities of living outside the modern industrialized world, a couple long plane rides can illustrate live and in 3-D what many of us only see on television.

When we take a look at the overall world we are living in, 1 billion people don't have clean running water. About 1.3 billion earn less than $1 a day and half the world population lives on less than $2 a day.

At the other end of the spectrum, a mere 6% of the planet's people control nearly 60% of the wealth.

Consequently, with so few puppeteering so much, 80% of the world's population lives in substandard housing and more than two of every three cannot read. Only one-in-four has a roof over their head, a place to sleep, clothes to wear and food in the refrigerator.

Well over half the world's population has never made a phone call and only about 7% are computer-literate and online.

Even more sobering, this week over a million ill and less fortunate than we will die in hunger and pain. Most know it – and have no agonizing choice but to await their inevitable turn.

The U.S., meanwhile, is not without its own set of quality of life challenges. Domestically, Marian Wright Edelman champions the cause of disadvantaged children through the United States from her office in Washington, D. C.

Marian is a Yale Law School graduate and author of five books, including the #1 New York Times bestseller, *"The Measure of Our Success: A Letter to My Children and Yours."*

After founding the Children's Defense Fund in 1973, Ms. Edelman's relentless fight to provide all children a protective start in life with the help of concerned families and communities has been unwavering.

In 2000, Ms. Edelman was awarded the nation's highest civilian honor – The Presidential Medal of Freedom – in recognition of her lifelong work helping others live better lives. With or without money, this is a very, *very* rich woman and wonderful role model for everyone who dreams of making a positive difference in the lives of others. Marian found her passion in life and is relentless in its pursuit.

Across the continent, tucked away in a low-profile office building in Seattle, Melinda Gates steers a staff of 200 overseeing a $23.5 billion asset base for the Bill & Melinda Gates Foundation. Their shared passion is world health.

"The loss of a child in one place on the planet is no less tragic than the loss of a child in another," Melinda said recently.

The Gates Foundation supplies vaccines to children in 74 countries, is helping eliminate epidemic meningitis in sub-Sahara Africa, and working diligently to help accelerate the global effort to create and distribute an AIDS vaccine.

To help further the cause, the Gates Foundation is also funding the investment in 20,000 minority college scholarships over the next 20 years to assist development of multi-cultural leadership across the nation. The price tag? A cool *one billion* dollars.

The Gates Foundation is doing its best to make the world smaller and better too.

So what does travel teach us? For the philanthropic, it opens up doors of opportunity to significantly change and improve the lives of others.

For those less financially able, it grounds us in the reality that *we already are far more fortunate* than billions of others. And given the watercolor of opportunity our lives and jobs have painted on the canvas before us, it's up to each one of us to pick up a paintbrush and paint the color that looks the best to finish the personal artwork we want to create.

Travel also reminds us that each nation and its people are their very own piece of art. And art appreciation is subjective, since beauty's in the eye of the beholder.

Nature, above all, champions the power of diversity. For example, if you've ever been in a zoo and seen a yak, they sure doesn't look like much – just a big hairy ox badly in need of a haircut, usually posing motionless like a stuffed animal in the Christmas display window at F.A.O. Schwartz.

But nature has important plans for everything – even the lowly yak. An even-toed hoofed animal weighing upward of 1,200 pounds, this lumbering woolly beast carries its head mopingly low and lives only in the high country of Tibet. Yaks are one of the world's rarest and oddest-looking beasts.

Glancing at one, you wouldn't think a yak's particularly good for much of anything. But in their role, they are the monarchs of the world's highest mountains. An agile beast despite its huskiness, the yak can slide down glaciers, swim rivers and leap over rocks.

Crossed with Mongolian cattle, they've carried the burdens of the Mongols and Sherpas for centuries. Without the yaks, the Sherpas cannot live in the Himalayas.

And without the Sherpas, no one summits Everest. Without the yak, no man reaches the top of the world – and climbing the top of the planet's highest mountain to stand on top of the earth is considered by many to be a human's most difficult achievement.

We're all in this together, folks. That's the Renoir beauty of it all.

Oh – there's one last thing I've noticed, too: Children all around the world are happy. They don't fear diversity because they haven't been taught any differently. Kids all around the world laugh and giggle and run around playing tag and hide-and-seek, while sliding down just about anything they can find that's remotely slide-able.

There's a reason, a very good reason, kids around the world are happy: Nobody ever told them they weren't supposed to be. A simple point worth committing to the soul.

There's a richness in living with the magical ability to look at the world through the eyes of a child regardless how many winters we've seen.

Words to live by, for sure.

Section Two:

THE
PRESENT

LIVIN' LIFE ON THE PRO LEISURE TOUR

Creating Your Daily Dozen

The Hourglass of Time

When to Switch Jobs

Thrivers, Survivors & Chevrolet Drivers

Success Probability

**What to do
When Things Go Wrong**

Chapter 3

LIVIN' LIFE ON THE PRO LEISURE TOUR
THE CARPET RIDE TO HAPPINESS

The Pro Leisure Tour is an attitude, a state of mind. Life "On Tour" doesn't require being retired. Far from it. Most members aren't. They make choices about how they act and how they think and what they choose to worry (or not worry) about. They live with a sense of balanced contentment.

Living Life on the Pro Leisure Tour is simply a conscious decision to emerge from the surrounding mayhem of each day's various distractions with a smile on your face, a bounce in your stride and the happy confidence that today's sundown means tomorrow will be here that much sooner.

One quick way to whittle some sadness out of life is to learn to minimize the time that _worry_ occupies during each day's waking hours.

That's what this chapter's about: What worry is, how to pro-actively manage it, and – most importantly – how to keep the gremlins from holding track meets in your head. PLT living includes learning how to manage these things and relocate them from the foreground of our consciousness to the background.

Life on the Pro Leisure Tour means being content, positive, and good to others. It's a lifestyle choice – an attitude – and this book contains the simple recipe.

Every minute of every hour of every day is worth living. From time-to-time some people seem to forget that – but folks on the PLT never do. They simply sign up to live the Tour's motto: _"Live Life. Love the Journey."_ And once signed-up, PLT-ers role-model it.

I often repeat what my old baseball friend Elden Auker always said about waking up in the morning: "Every day's a good day if

35

you're on the right side of the green." Nearly 70 years after surrendering home runs 691 and 701 to Babe Ruth, and 60 years after nearly stopping Joe DiMaggio's famed 56-game hitting streak at 35, Elden still loves every single sunrise.

What really matters internally then, isn't the *result* of living so much as the journey.

The *journey* matters.

Years ago, during that quixotic suspension-bridge crossing from college graduate to real adult, I was stopped in my tracks one evening by a female friend who asked me one very simple and direct question.

As I paused to drop her off in front of her apartment, she looked at me and asked simply, "Are you happy?"

I thought about my answer for several uncomfortable seconds because the question seemed be one of those dangerous "right answer, wrong answer" types.

After a long and uneasy silence, I finally slowly and uncertainly told her the truth the best I knew it. "I don't know," I replied. "What is it?"

She took that answer as a "no." And soon, I was in the rear-view mirror of her life. She knew what happiness was and had no interest in wasting her time with men who didn't.

Happiness proved to be a learned thing for me. It was another one of those blasted things they forgot to teach in school. I remember thinking about her question – and my answer – a thousand different times over the next few years. And for all the overflowing bushel baskets full of cash I spent grinding and bleeding my way through college, the *least* they could've done was teach me *everything* I needed to learn during the four years I showed up and tried to pay attention.

That was an uneasy time for me. I was hurt I got dumped by someone half my size; and worse, I was uncomfortable I couldn't truthfully smile and answer her question with a quick and emphatic, "Heck, *yes*, I'm happy!"

A lot of living has since passed by. A lot of joy but a lot of funerals, too. Too many. Despite life's sporadic storm clouds and raindrops of sorrow, I'm now convinced that happiness is a choice.

Happiness starts with answering for yourself that innocuous little question I wrestled so uncomfortably with. If you struggle for a truthful answer – and don't like the one you end up with – well, welcome to The Road to Oz. The hard part is finding the yellow brick road. Following it is a lot easier than locating it in the first place.

Happiness is pretty broad-spectrumed. On one hand, there are the happy-all-the-time always-grinning extremists. These folks are happy all the time no matter *what* happens. They could sneeze the nose right off their face and blow the house down and they'd still be grinning from ear-to-ear because the TV was still standing amidst the rubble. Don't get me wrong: I'm all *for* happiness – but *controlled* happiness.

Then, on the other hand, you've got people who totally eschew materialistic possessions. They say the secret to happiness is easy: Want nothing. If you want nothing, you should automatically be happy all the time.

These extremes puzzle me. I vote for a much more practical comfort zone between the two.

Some folks only smile when they're what I call *"work happy."* Work Happy is the fake happiness mask too many people wear in the office. I know a lot of pretty miserable people who smile at work but don't mean it. They grin from 8-to-5 but once they leave the office, they don't smile again until they return for showtime the following day. Some even wrestle with depression. Smile on the outside, cry on the inside. Their emotional rowboat has capsized.

So, what really *is* happy, besides an adjective? The dictionary definition is: *"Favored by circumstances; lucky; fortunate. Having, showing or causing a feeling of great pleasure, contentment or joy."*

What's the key word in that definition? Pause for a moment, read it again and decide for yourself. What one word inside that definition is the most important?

Have you picked one out?

I think the most important word is *"causing."* Causing is the action word – the *catalyst* of creating a wonderfully positive result. Causing, then, is action-oriented.

Everyone on the Pro Leisure Tour is expected to commit random acts of kindness whenever the whim strikes and for no reason at all. Mark Twain once said, "The best way to cheer yourself up is to cheer everybody else up." There's a childlike purity in the joy good deeds will bring. Try a few and see.

Let's take a very quick look at one other synonym for the word *"happy."* Let's look at the root-word for "contentment" – *"content."*

The dictionary definition is worth memorizing, or at least writing down as a reminder. Contentment is a key component to living life on The Pro Leisure Tour.

Muhammad Ali is one of the most content people I've ever seen, a brilliant role model for inner peace. Muhammad's happiness is no accident. He's got a recipe for living we all should admire and emulate. Deep down, despite his middle-aged medical challenges, Muhammad's a very content individual.

"Content," also an adjective – a description word that means: *"Happy enough with what one has or is; not desiring something more or different; satisfied."*

There is tremendous power in this simple definition. Once you own and embrace this succinct description, you will be in the middle ground between needing more and wanting less.

The motivation industry has become an enormous umbrella of umbrage for millions of people looking for help with life and career guidance – a massive industry unto itself. But why? Why has the business of motivation even evolved, much less mushroomed so dramatically? Why are some people motivated and some aren't? Why are some happy and some aren't?

Two main reasons:

1. Many people live a life that's out-of-balance. *Way out-of-balance in some cases.*

Compared to a life that's in-balance, people who haven't sat back, analyzed their feelings and emotions and happiness quotient ("HQ") face a long uphill walk to contentment. This is common because it's normal. People can bury themselves in one aspect of life and ignore the others for a myriad of reasons: Escapism, hunger for recognition, fear, ego – the list goes on and on.

Consider life to be plate-spinning on-stage. You are the entertainer and all your family and friends are seated in the audience. A row of tall flexible rods, each with a plate on top, stands before you. Your job as a professional plate spinner is to keep each plate spinning atop its individual rod without falling off and crashing to the floor.

One spinning plate represents your job.

The next is your cherished tax-return co-signer.

Then there are the kids (and each gets his or her very own plate).

The next several plates represent your extended family, your friends, money you need to save, bills you need to pay, your health, your hobbies, your civic duties to help others – well, the row of plates can go clear across the stage. At the end, feel free to spin an extra plate that represents all the things you'd like to do but never have the time to get to.

Your life is running back and forth, vibrantly and decisively shaking the rods of the plates that wobble the most to get them spinning smartly and safely again.

Whew. No wonder plates wobble off the sticks and crash on the floor.

Work is 24% of your life – less than one-fourth. Treat it that way. And if work is only one-fourth of your life, what's non-work? The vast majority, right?

For many people around the world, work grows into more than simply a vehicle to pay the bills. It's an identity, a yardstick of personal achievement, or a workaholic refuge to hide from the sometimes-demanding social interactions of marriage, parenting, or community involvement.

This absolute compulsion to work is globally understood. Having viewed societies and cultures from all around the world, I'm tempted to agree with the worn out cliché that too many people live to work rather than work to live.

In order to be truly happy, you have to live a life where you're rich __without__ money. I know several miserable millionaires. It's a perplexing thing to watch someone with the business acumen or financial wherewithal to do whatever in life they choose – and yet be totally so clueless at understanding the simple ingredients of happiness.

Just as tragic, I've also lost a friend whose reasons for living apparently drowned alongside a failed business venture.

If you focus on staying rich internally – regardless of the peaks and valleys of a fluctuating bank account – you'll always stay centered.

2. Besides out-of-balance lifestyles, adults not living life on the Pro Leisure Tour seem to specialize in worrying.

They worry incessantly – about nearly everything. Worrying is like a demanding second-job they faithfully attend – never missing a day. Some people even seem to be in a contest to see how much they can worry about. If the Olympics declared "Worrying" a sport, the U.S. team be formidable favorite to sweep the medals.

Since living life on The Pro Leisure Tour is all about maintaining emotional balance and contentment, let's just take a quick look at two words I often hear from people who are struggling to snap out of their funk and doldrums. Both words are temporary barriers preventing them from getting where they need to go.

One is *"empty."* I hear that one a lot. In the human emotional context, this adjective means: *"Having no worth or purpose; useless or unsatisfying; without meaning."*

Empty lives listlessly waste precious days. Lives with a purpose waste none. Days are a non-renewable resource. Wasting them is a crime. Wasting one is a misdemeanor. Wasting many, well, that's more like a personal felony.

The second barrier word is *"sad."* Sad means *"having, expressing, or showing low spirits or sorrow; unhappy."*

Look, let's face the obvious – no one is happy all the time. Life's too tough for that. But no one should be sad all the time, either. Life's got too many good things to offer. Sadness needs to be a temporary storm cloud that gusts of positive wind can quickly blow away.

Mickey Rivers Was Right

And what *is* worry? At the risk of wearing out the dictionary, its definition sounds familiar: *"To feel distressed in the mind; be anxious, troubled, or uneasy."*

Put simply, *worrying* is sending your mind into the future and *fantasizing* trouble or *imagining* potential problems. You think and fear things that *might* happen.

Worry is a very negative fantasy, as opposed to a dream – which is a very positive one. If you want to send your mind on ahead and focus on an imaginary future, which would seem to be more worthwhile to ponder? A negative fantasy or a positive one?

So, worry creates stress through fantasizing future possibilities. And anger is the stress emotion. Depression *also* bubbles up from the lava flow of internalized stress.

41

What happens if you worry too much about things that probably won't happen?

When people spend too much time fantasizing negativity, sure as winter rain in Seattle one the following things is likely to happen:

- Either they finally realize it's a colossal waste of time to worry about the improbable;
- They procrastinate;
- They reach a panic point and start to hurriedly build a plan; or,
- Worst of all, they do nothing. Their worries run haphazardly through their mind like the bulls thundering loose through the streets of Pamplona. And, like Pamplona, many good people end up getting trampled for no good reason at all.

When Logic Starts Leaking, Turn off the Valve

Many people quickly learn that they <u>have</u> the power to recognize and consciously shut off negative and hypothetical thoughts.

The worst of worrisome thinking often focuses on remote possibilities that have a very low chance of *ever* occurring. People often get consumed by wildly overreacting to the worst possible thing that *could* happen – even though it probably never would.

If something probably *never* will happen, why burn a stressful and consuming amount of negative energy pretending it will? Doing so makes little sense.

One good option is giving hypothetical thoughts a quick boot right out the ear canal as soon as they arrive. Police your own mind. If something's not a fact – don't treat it like one.

Procrastination: **Life's Toll Booth to Everywhere**

Procrastinators *will* practice their specialty. The world is *full* of procrastinators.

Why? Is procrastination a genetic trait? A lifelong condemnation? Should thumb-twiddling and doing nothing be an acceptable career path? Of course not!

People procrastinate for a trio of reasons: They lack attainable goals worth pursuing; don't value their time; or are stymied to figure out their next step forward.

♦ *Goals, <u>written</u> goals, are part of the prescription for every procrastinator.*

In our next chapter, you'll have the opportunity to script a dozen goals of your own. A simple exercise will steer you to jot down and scrutinize who you aspire to be in life. It's a good soul-searching exercise you'll enjoy completing.

Remember: A goal is a dream with a deadline. We all need written goals in life – at home and in the office. Reaching them always brings a flood of positive-feeling endorphins.

♦ *People who don't value their time never reach half their life's potential.*

Creating a sense of urgency for living cures that. How that urgency gets kick-started comes from a wheelbarrow full of different ways. Each of us can learn the true, absolute value of time one of two ways: Proactively or reactively.

Proactive awareness comes from watching, reading, learning, and doing. For most people, personal achievement fuels the desire for *additional* achievement. Lack of achievement does the same thing in reverse. People who've never tasted worthwhile, hard-earned success don't realize that what they're missing is sweeter than sugar.

Pro golfer, businessman extraordinaire and outdoor adventure-seeker Greg Norman is anything *but* a procrastinator. His life motto is succinct and to the point: *"Attack Life!"*

Norman lives each jam-packed day with an extraordinary energy and urgency and deals with the realities of life as it unfolds each day before him. Part of his secret is he has no fear of making decisions and making things happen.

Norman's a great role model for people who aspire to squeeze more fun and action into life. Norman manages his time brilliantly, investing huge chunks while wasting very little.

Many aren't like Norman; they don't learn to attack life proactively and end up learning to do it *reactively*. Often a significant emotional event in life jars people into cherishing the finite inventory of limited life moments they've been allocated.

In my case, life changed forever when I saw video footage of a private plane crash one night on the evening news. A close friend was the pilot. Hours before, we had finished 18 holes of golf together and hugged goodbye. I headed for my car, and he was heading for his plane.

We spent half that tragic day candidly discussing life, living and family – all the things close friends talk about in private when they finally get the chance.

That news broadcast jarred me like a lightning bolt. From that instant to this, never has a day gone by that I don't try to achieve things of value either for my family, friends, self or others. I learned better how to live while helplessly watching his family deal with a tragically devastating and irrevocable loss.

Sometimes that's what happens. Sometimes the habit of procrastination – and that's all it is, *a habit* – ends at the stinging tip of a thunderbolt hurled angrily from the powerful arm of the God of Reality. The God of Reality has a strong arm and good aim. He hits people in the butt with those things every single day.

♦ **_Lastly, sometimes lacking a sense of urgency isn't the procrastinator's biggest problem._**

People often fiddle around doing nothing simply because they don't know what to do next. Where do they start? What's the best first step?

Either they *can't* do something; *won't* do it; or are *prevented from* doing it. In a later chapter, we'll dissect all three of these scenarios (*can't, won't* and *prevented from*) and learn quick fixes for each – effective remedies for both home and office.

People who worry about what <u>*might*</u> *happen* tend to be less action-oriented than those who step-up and deal with realities at-hand. While we can't change human nature and eliminate procrastination, we certainly can (and will) learn to effectively manage it.

Protect the Fort & Call out the Cavalry

Sometimes what we worry about has a *better-than-average probability* of occurring. Then the best option is accepting it as a downslide of life's rollercoaster, and deciding to battle it with a pro-active plan.

Fuel the construction of your plan with the conscious creation of endorphins. Endorphins are powerful things and, best of all, easily self-created. By accepting the impending event as a challenge, you minimize the fear. Never forget what General George S. Patton said about the difference between courage and fear: "Courage is fear holding on a moment longer."

Channeled worry becomes fear only if you don't step up and deal with it. Stepping up, analyzing all options, picking the best one, and implementing actions converts former fear directly into new-found courage.

There is a great strength that comes from taking action. You'll feel it flow through every corpuscle.

Real challenges and stresses in life are normal. We all have them. But, like anyone caught in stormy seas in a small boat knows, there are two ways to deal with rough water: Close your eyes and hope for the best (stay fearful and reactive); or point the bow of the boat head-on into the waves and ride it out (be courageous and proactive). Very small boats can survive very large storms simply by point their bows to the wave.

Always point the bow of your life into the waves.

The Dumbest Thing of All: *Taking The Ostrich Approach*

The final option, of course, is simply letting worries run wild. Free range, unencumbered by fences or boundaries, worries multiply like street rats. They take different shapes, degrees of severity (usually worsening by the day) and seem to accelerate the speed of their frantic and repetitive laps around the brain.

Worrying can get totally exhaustive – physically *and* emotionally. Negative *"what if"* thinking can be endless – if you let it. The best way to control your worries is simply by:

♦ *Deciding* what (if anything) truly is worth worrying about.

♦ *Recognizing* the factual cause.

♦ *Identifying* the most pragmatic remedy.

♦ *Taking action steps* to address a legitimate problem head-on.

Pearls of Wisdom from Mick the Quick

Former New York Yankee outfielder and famed non-worrier Mickey Rivers once explained why he always seemed so care-free. Mick the Quick never seemed to worry about much of anything at all. In baseball circles, he got sort of famous for it.

"Ain't no sense worryin' 'bout stuff you got no control over," Rivers once told a reporter, "Cause if you got no control over it, there ain't no sense worryin.'"

The reporter squinted, shook his head sideways, and stared at Rivers like a dog watching television. He didn't have a clue what Rivers just said, but it all made perfect sense to Mickey.

And Mickey was right. If you *can't* control something, why fantasize about it in a negative way? Why torch your own house with imaginary worst-case scenarios replayed in your mind over and over and over again, the flames burning higher and higher every time you replay what *might* happen? To do so is utterly pointless.

Mickey Rivers simplified things two ways: Either he *could* control something or he couldn't. If he *could* control it, he didn't worry because he had confidence in his ability to deal with whatever cards reality dealt.

If Rivers *couldn't* control something, Mick refused to burn energy pondering hypothetical what-ifs that probably would never happen. If it was something he couldn't change, he sure wasn't going to lose one minute of life pretending he could.

Mick's advice is 24-carat gold. Well worth taking. If you *can* control something, then analyze your options rationally, focus on the best course of action, and take it. Don't just *think* about the best solution – be pro-active *and take it!* By doing so, *you* will be managing the stress rather than having the stress manage *you*.

Never forget: The only things in life <u>you</u> have control over are things you do yourself. If someone else can influence the outcome, *<u>you</u> do not* have control. Minimize the things you worry about that you cannot control. Focus on the things you can.

The White Knights & Dr. Feelgood

It's very common that people who get all bogged down in stress and worry often fail to realize they've got a tag-team partner waiting patiently in their corner to tag-in and leap over the ring ropes to help combat the bad guys.

Each of us has what's called an Autonomic Nervous System (ANS) that releases adrenaline and endorphins automatically. The

ANS is not something any of us consciously controls. It's a reflex system built-in to automatically trigger reflex responses to save our lives.

Besides adrenaline and endorphins, the ANS triggers things like stress responses, worry and worrisome thoughts, fear, terror, anxiety, accelerations in blood pressure, increased heart rates, nervous sweats, hand tremors, and a myriad of other things.

Science says endorphins are neurotransmitters naturally released in the brain following aerobic exercise, romantic intimacy, or laughter – and any combination thereof. And if science says it, well, it must be true!

Endorphins are the body's natural antidepressants. They produce more white blood cells – and white blood cells do two important things for you simultaneously:

1. They deter depression, *and*

2. They bolster the immune system.

To show how endorphins are produced, let's take a quick look at one of the their three common releases: Laughter. Laughter is generated as a byproduct of comedic communication. And effective communication requires four things: A sender, receiver, message and medium of conveyance.

As a youth, I didn't know any of that. But I did find myself at a very young age captivated by the work of the geniuses of the Golden Era of comedy. These included Mack Sennett's Keystone Cops, Buster Keaton, W.C. Fields, Ben Turpin, Harold Lloyd, Fatty Arbuckle and the greatest of them all, Charles Chaplin. They introduced me to my first million endorphins without me even knowing it.

After learning about visual humor from comedy's silent era, I studied the comedic impact of the written and spoken word from the verbal choices, word order, setups, delivery and timing of Groucho Marx and Jack Benny. Plus, I carefully watched the choreographed teamwork of Gracie Allen and her life-long straight man and husband, George Burns.

And, of course, the fearless courage of Johnny Carson was exhibited during the opening seven-minute monologue of every late night show he did. Jack Benny, incidentally, was one of Carson's role models. Carson thought Benny's sense of comedic timing was brilliant – the best in the world – and he crafted much of his personal style by studying and applying what made Benny so intrinsically special.

During the comedy industry's Golden Era of silent films, endorphins were released by laughs generated by visual imagery. The floodgates were controlled by a transition from the eyes to the brain and that was how comedians built their messages: Sight gags.

Generating laughs via silent films was totally different than radio. Radio sent the message through the auditory canals to the brain. The laughter came from what the audience heard and imagined – not what they saw.

Throughout the silent film era, people traditionally learned and laughed from an ocular stimulus – their eyes carried the message to the brain. Movies and newsreels were filmed specifically with direct visual imagery.

With radio, learning came through the ears. Spoken words were used to paint pictures on the canvas of the listener's imagination.

But talking pictures (and eventually television) were different. When talking pictures came into being, the entertainment industry suddenly spun on its axis. Comedy was forced into another evolutionary metamorphosis. The medium to deliver the message had changed completely. Talkies and TV demanded a merging of separate yet integrated sources of comedic stimulus: Messages now needed to be sent (and choreographed) to both the eyes *and* ears.

The spoken word – not *just* a visual message – quickly evolved into the theatre's primary endorphin trigger. The men and women who created the world's laugher shifted the wheelhouse controls to laughter's floodgates from the eyes to the ears. This change was perfectly suited to the extraordinary blend of physical and verbal skills owned by the brilliant comedienne Lucille Ball.

Two of the industry's four communication components changed – the message *and* delivery channel – but the other two, the sender and receiver, did not. The sender and receiver remained the filmmaker and the audience.

Yet while the mediums changed completely – the entertainers' objective did not. Their goal never changed: Create a controlled, streaming release of endorphins by generating repetitive laughter.

It's no accident comedy is such a powerful force and multi-billion-dollar global industry unto itself. Laughter releases endorphins and endorphins make you feel better. They do so for a very good reason: Endorphins use the same human receptor sites as most morphine-based narcotics.

Laughter, then, creates pretty much its own natural narcotic. Try being unhappy with a smile on your face – *it's impossible!* Laughter is great stuff and its importance in our lives should never be underestimated or taken for granted. It's a very necessary ingredient of living a happy life on The Pro Leisure Tour.

Along with laughter, aerobic exercise – including sex – also produces endorphins to create the same "feel good" type of positive and happy emotional state. So can positive adrenaline.

Generally, it takes a good 20-minute workout for endorphins to release. And if you make the time to relax after your workout – choosing not to go jump immediately into something else – the post-release narcotic effect will last another 20 minutes or so, as well. In other words, a 20-minute post-exercise relaxation period will maximize your feel-good experience.

Exercise also can have a 24-hour residual effect, which is why so many people respond positively to physical exercise. The improved attitude is not a coincidence. It comes directly from a biological infusion of feel-good medicine right into the brain.

Many frazzled people don't even realize that Dr. Feelgood is always standing by in times of need. Endorphins wear running, hiking, and walking shoes. If they are in your closet, so is Dr. Feelgood.

Coupling the power of exercise with released endorphins creates a natural antidepressant and anti-anxiety treatment. Even better, anxiety and depression can't live in an endorphined-alpha-state.

So, if 20 minutes of exercise followed by a 20-minute relaxation period can help ward off negative thought and emotion, clearly it's a modest personal investment that pays spectacular dividends.

Teaming up to engage your ANS with your CNS (Central Nervous System) strengthens you quickly, both emotionally *and* physically. The ANS steers your emotional reflexes while your CNS controls your physical motors. Together, they'll team up to combat negativity.

Best of all, releasing endorphins is totally controllable. *You* can choose to set them free whenever you want. Pick the potions that create the best mix for your personal treasure chest: Exercise, laughter, romance or adrenaline.

All are ingredients in the prescription for life on The Pro Leisure Tour. Everyone has their own elixir of those four important things that generate good feelings.

They cost nothing. No credit card and month of expiration required.

Appreciate the power of endorphins and know that in tough times they are housed within you and always ready to help locate the light at the far end of the tunnel.

Learning *how* to feel good is important. But so is learning how to *avoid* feeling bad. Another key part of Living Life on the PLT is learning to manage what you worry about and what you won't. Doing so is much easier than most folks realize.

"The Worry Circle"

"You cannot prevent the birds of sorrow from flying over your head, but you can prevent them from building nests in your hair."
- Chinese Proverb

Worry doesn't *fix* anything. Never does. It'll drive you nuts, but it sure won't help make anything better.

One of my closest friends, a retired business executive and compulsive neat-freak named Dick Haase, offered me a theory many years ago I never forgot. I nicknamed Haase "Huevos," which is Spanish for "egg." Golf reasons, since Huevos never met a sand trap he couldn't hit into and every time we looked at his ball in the sand, it always seemed to be sitting there looking like a fried egg. Huevos was an omelet maker, dressed in funny shoes and odd clothes.

Huevos was convinced that human nature requires that we worry about something all the darn time. Worrying, in his view, was a mandatory part of living – just like inhaling and exhaling. He named his theory *"The Worry Circle."* And contained inside The Worry Circle are all the things each of us, individually, tends to worry about.

It's a simple theory but one that's hard to debate. Clearly, we all *do* worry about things. *What* we worry about changes over time.

But Huevos wasn't concerned about *what* we worry about. He was simply convinced that it was human nature to worry and human nature wouldn't let any of us go so much as a single day without worrying.

If you solved a problem or eliminated something you'd been worrying about, human nature immediately compelled something new to pop up inside the circle and take a place among its worrisome brethren. Solved worries were always replaced by new ones.

Huevos said The Worry Circle must remain full at all times. Keeping it full was simply human nature.

I bought the concept. Years later, I still do. Now I talk about The Worry Circle freely – sort of like it's as much a part of a person as a nose, navel or fingernail.

The Worry Circle exists. But the art of Pro Leisure Tour Living is managing The Circle to your advantage, rather than having the nefarious Circle hammerlock you into submission.

The next few pages teach you how.

Managing "The Worry Circle"

Prudent Worry Circle management requires remembering what Mickey Rivers said. If you've got no control over something, then why should you worry about it? Why worry about uncontrollables? Rather unnecessary burnt energy, isn't it?

Some folks have larger Worry Circles than others – and size *does* matter – but everyone agrees in one form or another The Circle exists.

Effectively managing your Worry Circle first requires identifying what has sneaked inside its permeable walls.

Our first step then (see the oval on the next page) is simply laundry-listing everything that worries you on a sheet of paper. Typically, the list is long and the circle gets filled. After all, each aspect of our lives generates its own set of concerns.

Do your best to fill up the exercise circle with as many things as you can possibly think of that are causing you stress. Spend the time to fill out the exercise with care. We'll step through a real-life example – yours – as the rest of the chapter unfolds.

Typical Things You're Worrying About

(fill in your own Worry Circle below)

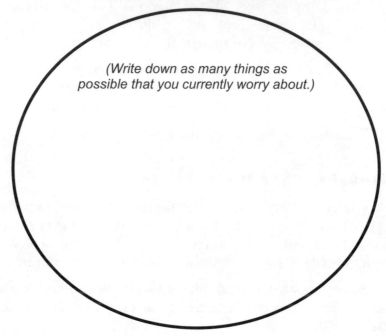

(Write down as many things as possible that you currently worry about.)

Once your Worry Circle (above) is complete and the issues are fully-identified, the next step involves stratifying its contents into two piles:

    *1) What you **Can** control, and*
    *2) What you **Can't**.*

This is usually where the fun starts. It's even more fun to watch people suddenly realize that so much of what they worry about are things they can't possibly ever hope to control. In most cases, over half of what we worry about are things we have absolutely no control over and never *will* have any control over.

Always remember that the only things we <u>can</u> control are those events we are directly involved in and that others cannot influence. On the following two pages, sort your list accordingly and transcribe your current worries into the appropriate circles.

The Worry Circle:

"Controllables" vs. "Uncontrollables"

From your completed Worry Circle (on the previous page), take each identified issue and put it in the appropriate Worry Circle (either below, if you have direct control over it; or on the following page if you don't).

Either you *can* control what you worry about or you *can't*. Now, sort each item from your previous master list appropriately.

Things You
CAN **CONTROL**

Everything inside the above circle should be things you (yourself) can fix, change, address, improve or eliminate. If they depend on the aid of others to resolve, they are *not* totally under your control and belong in the circle on the next page.

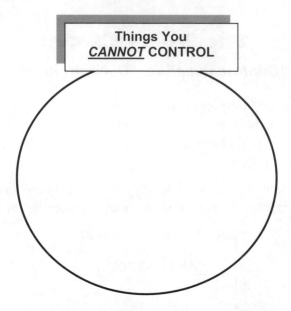

With the contents of your original Worry Circle now accurately divided into these two separate repositories, the next step is simple: *All the issues that are Uncontrollable are kicked out of The Circle – for good.* Psychologically, they're banished from the precious real estate between our ears.

If we _CAN'T_ control something, we simply *refuse* to burn wasted energy worrying about it!

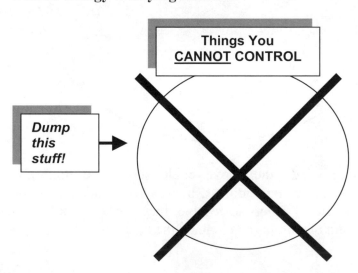

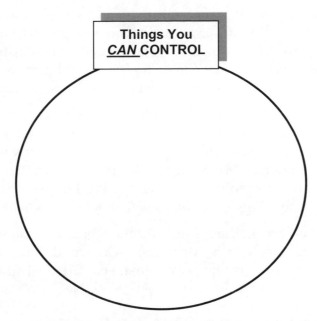

Things You
CAN CONTROL

Our total focus now shifts to what's left – those things inside the circle you've identified as things you can specifically influence yourself: Things you *can* control.

These identified controllables are what we'll channel our energies toward addressing. It's for these remaining concerns that we will plan and build solutions.

There is a method, a process, you'll soon learn to quickly build confident and positive solutions for each of the issues still remaining encircled.

Once you've got the confidence to deal with anything within your control, what you worry about quickly diminishes, then disappears, like melting springtime snow. Stress is fueled by the lack of visible remedies. Once plans emerge to deal with problems at-hand, stress levels diminish.

For now, let's simply embrace the belief that worrying is normal. If you're human – you'll worry. But let's also embrace the belief that a key ingredient of contented living on The Pro Leisure Tour is worrying *only* about those things we have direct control over.

57

Each one of us lives with a unique set of worries totally different than everyone else walking, crawling, or wheeling his or her way around the planet. The shared commonality is the existence of The Worry Circle itself; our uniqueness is what's inside our own personal Circle and how we choose to deal with it.

Life between the ears can be hard or easy, depending on how you consciously decide to live it. As you may have noticed from past experience, the world can get heavy in a hurry if you insist on carrying it around. Managing the Worry Circle sure helps lighten the load. There's too much fun on The Pro Leisure Tour to waste time and energy lugging around a planet full of dirty laundry.

On The Pro Leisure Tour, we much prefer whistling off-key and singing poorly to heavy lifting. The world, quite frankly, is just too darn cumbersome to tote around day after exhausting day.

What You've Got vs. What You Don't

Always remind yourself to be grateful for what you have – never worry about what you don't. Embracing those simple words are like removing the heavy oaken yoke from a plow oxen. A great weight is lifted, and life is suddenly better.

No one can have it all; and if you did – what would be the point of continuing on?

That simple saying will also automatically become a protective strainer helping to guard the Worry Circle perimeter of your very own life. By shielding the irrelevant from entry, there's never a need to expend the energy to kick the irrelevant right back out.

8 G-r-r-r-reat Tips for Living Life on The PLT:

1. Focus on the facts.

Don't fear the hypothetical. Factual things we can methodically and systematically deal with by roadmapping sound solutions. Hypothetical "what ifs" are boundless and a colossal waste of time. Don't chase trick emotional rainbows. They never end and you'll never catch one.

2. *Never – ever – doubt your ability to do something that's within your capabilities.*

Lightning bolts of doubt are fear's tattoos. Courage is fear held out a bit longer, so never willingly step on the downward escalator toward giving up. PLT Living includes being productive with your time and energies and a key ingredient in that is assured confidence. Few things worth doing are easy. But if you dream of something truly is worth doing – or trying – don't worry about failure. Be like Nike. *Just do it.*

3. *Ignore the past.*

You can't live in it, can't change it and, above all, you can't control it. But what you can and should do is learn from it. If you cling to the past – for good reasons or bad – you'll never be fully-focused on today or tomorrow. The PLT is a present-tense society, so cherish the challenges of every sunrise.

4. *Live in one-day cocoons.*

Part of becoming a butterfly is first being a caterpillar. The greatest feats in engineering history – from Stonehenge to Hoover Dam – all started with one single and very-determined shovel of moved dirt.

5. *Stay busy.*

If you stay busy, you have no time to worry. Worrisome thoughts mushroom from idle time like sparks from a lit Roman candle. Busy people create the most endorphins (a primary fuel for the PLT). Also remember that the best ways to stay busy are to keep learning, doing for others, teaching and/or mentoring. It's hard to teach something to someone without learning something yourself.

6. *Doing your best always brings you a proud peace of mind.*

It's very much like performing a good hard day of work. When your ANS *(Autonomic Nervous System)* and CNS *(Central Nervous System)* are dance partners, you'll have a splendid peace of mind.

This is why top performers – in life, business, *and* society – typically are happy people and looked up-to by others. They exude positive, confident feelings. They're content with who they are, what they have a passion for and how they go about pursuing it. Contentment is a hall pass to living life on The Pro Leisure Tour.

7. ***Life on the PLT means managing the Worry Circle.***
   Here are five quick stress tips to help you out:
   a) *Only worry about things you can directly control.* Don't stray from that discipline.

   b) *Say no.* You can't be all things to all people. Never can be; never will. If you can't, or won't, do something, say so immediately and move on.

   c) *Identify your controllable stress triggers and what you can do to minimize them.* Know what your stress triggers are and pro-actively squish them. Ward them off ahead of time.

   For example, if certain things are an Achilles heel for your emotions (ex: lack of a clean house, punctuality, or money management) accept it and immediately commit to doing whatever's necessary to proactively eliminate those triggers from rearing their ugly, stressful heads.

   d) *Learn to delegate.* Don't *dump* – instead, *delegate.* Also remember that when you delegate, make sure to empower the recipient to own the project.

   e) *Make, then take, private time for yourself.* Make and invest fulfilling personal time for *JUST* yourself. Avoid, like a rattlesnake, being trapped into living a glass-walled sound-bite lifestyle. Plan time for you – and take it.

8. ***And, lastly, <u>always keep things in perspective!</u>***
   No matter *what* happens, well, four billion people around the world just won't care. It's sort of like the old adage concerning minor and major surgery. Minor surgery is what happens to others and major surgery is what happens to you.

None of us should take ourselves too seriously since our past means less than the opportunities of today and tomorrow. The late John Lennon, after the Beatles broke up, had this to say when he looked back on what the group achieved throughout their many historic years together: "We were a really good band," he said. "That's it. That's all it was. We were just a good band."

Lennon, of course, lived his entire life in the present and never looked back. He worried about little in life except his music, political beliefs and, a few years before he died, his family. Lennon's magic was his innate ability to transfer the feeling of the moment into a shared musical language everyone understood. As the times changed, so did he.

Lennon was never the same man waking up in the morning that he was the night before and no rule says any of us must be either. To him, today was yesterday's tomorrow and Lennon always lived for today – never for yesterday and never for tomorrow. He worried about things he could directly impact but very little else.

John had *concerns* beyond his immediate control, but very few worries. Importantly, he understood the difference between the two.

Nearly everything we worry about in life will eventually pass like streamwater parting past the bow of a smooth-gliding canoe. Don't panic when you see some whitewater. Pick your line, make a confident commitment where you're headed, and carefully steer your canoe through life's occasional rapids. If you do, you'll arrive nice and dry at your final destination.

Summary

Living Life on the Pro Leisure Tour means demonstrating the daily ability to cause and create contentment for those whose lives you have the opportunity to touch.

It means managing the Worry Circle, turning on your endorphin faucets full throttle as often as possible (and whenever necessary), and spicing your life with an occasional shot of

61

adrenaline because *it* provides the music that invites your ANS and CNS to dance a beautiful waltz.

Living on the Pro Leisure Tour also means signing up to commit random acts of kindness – not because Mark Twain said it's good to do but because you know it is.

And, Life on the PLT means you've chosen to live with the confidence of knowing *how* to sort out the controllable from the uncontrollable. In a following chapter, you'll soon learn how to quickly create smart plans to solve those controllable challenges.

Once you've got a solid plan, all that's left to do is confidently step forward and flawlessly execute the necessary action steps. When you take those steps and follow your plan, you'll quickly realize that there's little in life that will pop up that you can't tackle with a very high degree of confidence.

Lastly, never – ever – forget the Pro Leisure Tour motto stems from the contentment of your inner peace: *"Live Life. Love the Journey."* Life needs to be lived, not watched, and you can't live it on a sofa. The journey was made to be loved, not constantly worried about.

Live Life. Love the Journey. And be good to others along the way.

Chapter 4

Creating Your Daily Dozen

Several years ago I was struggling with a lot of cerebral confusion and escaped from my leveraged-to-the-nose home in Miami to a tiny island of refuge 50 miles away – Bimini in the Bahamas.

I went over to be alone and sort some things out. I knew I needed more focus in life – a clearer vision of who I wanted to be. I was searching, and knew it.

Sitting on the seawall by North Bimini's narrow harbor inlet, I sketched out a laundry list of brief phrases onto a scrap of paper. The challenge was attempting to define who I wanted to be, rather than who I really was.

The results of that head-to-heart with myself are now typed and laminated on a small card near where I write each day. I named that list "The Daily Dozen."

The Daily Dozen was a prioritized list of 12 things I identified to try and restore some balance into a life that was (at that time) clearly skewed uncomfortably *out* of balance. I was internally restless, knew it, and wanted to fix it.

My first Daily Dozen gave me a sorely-needed, self-created personal rudder. And since I was the one who authored the list – then prioritized the 12 specific points in order of importance after much careful thought and consideration – it was tough for me to argue its personal value.

The personal Daily Dozen ended up being such a help I developed a second one – a different one – for business. Business goals change all the time so I knew I needed a different one to complement the list I'd created for daily living. The two tie together nicely and symbiotically feed each other.

Why bother? Why take the time to create and write down two lists – one for business and another for life outside the office?

Simple.

Once you've created both lists and defined who you want to be at home and in the office, you've created a game plan to guide your future. Living becomes much simpler when you've got a *written* behavioral road map to follow, as needed. Writing these ideals down is very important. You can't just keep them between the ears.

We all have a mental list of things we don't do. For example, some people smoke, some don't. Some people are criminals, most aren't. Some criminals, however, don't smoke – they think it's bad for their health. Most of us don't rob banks, use heroin or intentionally hurt others.

So, since all of us have mental lists of things we *don't* do, why not create a couple *written* lists of important traits describing who we want to be?

As trite as it sounds, I often tell folks that life is what you do between shaves. When I reached a point of inner discontentment when I looked in my morning shaving mirror and carefully studied who was looking back, I knew it was time to do one of two things: Procrastinate and worry about it tomorrow – or step up and fix it.

I decided to fix it. If something in your life is troubling you, then step up and fix it. In my case, I sat on a Bahamian seawall and invested a couple priceless hours reshaping and bettering the rest of my life.

Your Daily Dozen is the backbone and ribcage for the core values you aspire to live by. All 12 ideals should be controllable. They will directly help solve fixable character flaws or improve on the core values that are most important to you.

Later in this chapter are easy-to-use worksheets to help step you through the creation of your own personal Daily Dozen.

Once you've created your Dozen, *post them somewhere you'll often see them!*

If *you* wrote them, and *you* see them, then *you'll* own them. Put your Daily Dozen somewhere plainly visible. The easier it is to see the list, the better.

If you write your personal Daily Dozen properly, all 12 are probably not going to real easy to live by. And they're not supposed to be.

Your Daily Dozen should <u>NOT</u> be a list detailing who you already are – but rather a realistic list of whom you aspire to be. It's a map of the road before you – not one with a little red dot that says *"You Are Here."*

By contrast, A Daily Dozen for business will be dynamic. If you invest the time to draw one up for work, expect your Business Dozen to change fairly often. But on a *personal* basis, if you've carefully thought through and crafted the dozen traits you most aspire to demonstrate, chances are your *personal* Daily Dozen will probably end up much like mine: It probably won't change much at all.

Remember to treat both lists – Personal and Business – as if they're written in pencil, not cement. They are goals and ambitions, not iron-clad mandates.

Although it's a bit close to the soul, I'll share my personal Dozen to help illustrate the point. This list was first written 10 years ago, the points culled and prioritized from 15 or 18 deeply-personal thoughts I had in Bimini. Over the last decade this small laminated card has served as a constant reminder of who I hope to be. As life changes, so might the list – but it hasn't yet.

Here's what I ended up with, and why. Note that all are written in the present tense for a very important reason. These are a dozen important personal traits I want to demonstrate *today* and they are listed in their stack-ranked order of importance to me.

The size of the gaps pursuing the achievement of each certainly has changed over time, but the importance of each ideal hasn't.

Ted's *Personal* Daily Dozen

1. Be a better husband. This is a hard one for me so it went deservedly to the very top of the list. Long-term relationships get bumpy. Being a great parent but lousy spouse is easy. But if you're a great spouse, it's pretty darn hard not to be a good parent, too.

2. Be a better father. I use the word "better" on purpose. I can't *be* perfect. Perfect is too hard. But I *can* be better. So can all of us, once we decide to.

3. Perform a quality day of work. Aristotle was right: "We are what we repeatedly do, excellence therefore is not an act but a habit."

Like many, by working full-time through college I learned that hard work and prudent time management enabled me to achieve as much or more in life than many people who finished school with far better grades but much less determination. I've always wanted my personal legacy to include a reputation as a hard-worker.

4. Eat sensibly. I'm a big guy and like groceries. Desserts sing to me. Unfortunately, I like *all kinds* of music.

5. Avoid alcohol. The older I get, the more I rue "the morning after." Too much time wasted. Lost time can never be recovered and, ironically, the only time the hands on the clock seemingly stop and refuse to budge are during a hangover or performance appraisal. Moderation is a better way.

6. Exercise. No two ways about it. You feel better *and* look better when you take the time to invest in yourself. I'm not a fanatic, simply aware of its importance and try to stay active.

It's hard to be emotionally sharp if you're physically unfit. The body is resilient, fitness can be achieved, and large victories emerge from small steps. It's never too late to begin a commitment to improved fitness.

7. Support my wife's personal growth. What's more fun than watching someone you care about learning, doing and achieving more in their lifetime? To me – not much.

8. Stay positive. I knew, deep down, I'd be better off if I became a "How Can I" person instead of being a "Can't Because" moaner and complainer. I'm so conscious of it now, I won't even utter the words "can't because" in a spoken sentence and an alarm goes off when I hear them.

9. Be nice. Shortly before I went over to sit by Bimini Harbour and think through all this stuff, Angelo Dundee, Muhammad Ali's Hall of Fame boxing trainer, sat me down in his office one day and lectured me on the importance of being nice to others.

I'm not too proud to admit that, for me, being nice was a learned skill. I had a chip on my shoulder bigger than a Chicago-style pizza until Angie's message finally got through.

10. Make a stranger laugh. Laughter is very important to me and has been since I was knee-high to a bullfrog.

Growing up, my heroes were the comic geniuses of my grandfather's era, not my own, and the laughter those performers created set endless magical endorphins gleefully free like a sky full of helium balloons of goodness.

By making the challenge of creating laughter for a perfect stranger a conscious part of every day, I remind myself how important laughter is in the life I want to live.

At the same time, making strangers laugh also means I'm taking Angelo's advice and being nice (*see #9, above*).

11. Pursue own personal growth. There's no personal fulfillment in going through life maintaining the status quo. When I wrote this one down, I had zero specific growth directions in mind but inherently realized I needed to consciously grow.

The pursuit of personal growth will steer its own course. Your needs and interests will lead you where your growth directions will head.

How I've grown over the last decade has changed, as will how I grow in the upcoming one. Same for all of us. What hasn't changed is the importance of continually challenging ourselves to keep climbing new ladders.

12. Write something. "A piece of paper's nothing 'til you write on it. What it is after that is up to you." I wrote that quote on the back of a business card while bouncing along on a Hertz shuttle bus late one night in Fresno.

That simple note best summarizes how I feel about crafting messages from consonants and vowels. I've always enjoyed the written expression of creative thought and put it 12th on my list to remind me that it's an important part of me – but not as important as the 11 others ahead of it.

Thoughts to Consider before Crafting **YOUR** "Daily Dozen"

Later in this chapter, I've included a series of simple charts to walk you through the process of creating your own personal Daily Dozen. Create your personal list first, then repeat the same techniques for your business Dozen if you wish.

As you begin thinking about what your Daily Dozen might include, remember that people with balance in life stand safely on the PLT balance beam and don't fall off.

Consider crafting your 12 key defining features around achieving a contented balance in life. For the sake of brainstorming, consider the *"Three Musketeers of Balance"* to be:

1. Physical. Give some thought to your physical well-being and the relative importance managing your personal fitness needs to play in the forming of the total person you hope to be.

2. Fiscal. Money and money-management can have a major (or minor) influence on your persona. Regardless of your style and values, be proactive with money management. In a committed relationship, it's vitally important to establish common financial ground. The number one cause of relationship discord is money. If you take that off the table – its stresses go with it.

Spending is one facet. Saving is another.

And what about giving? If you give 'til it hurts, then the depth of what you've given will bring a joy commensurate to that of the recipient. Giving away only things you don't need isn't nearly as fulfilling as giving much more. Giving more than what's easy creates the second best pain the world – next to childbirth.

Some folks are more materialistic than others. Wanting less makes it easier to give more.

Carefully consider all facets of personal economics and decide which, if any, might be worth capturing in your Daily Dozen listing.

3. *The Final Musketeer is Cerebral (and Emotional).*

Read. Experience. See. Feel. And do. Cerebral growth is why diversity works – it force-feeds the learning of different perspectives. Reading helps by expanding your vocabulary.

Most people regularly use less than 4% (only 15,000) of the 450,000 words in the English language. A mere 2,300 words are all anyone needs to learn to become English-conversant.

If you knew no English at all – and learned just two words a day, you'd be conversant in three years.

The more you read, the greater your vocabulary and the better you'll communicate. Your effectiveness in many aspects of living improves – at work, home, and in pursuit of hobbies and interests. You might also become a role model to others without even knowing it.

Cerebral growth and stimulation – however you choose to pursue it – is an important thing to consider when you sit down to sketch out the top 12 traits you truly aspire to demonstrate.

The Magic Formula

There *is* no magic formula or "Perfect Twelve" when building a Daily Dozen. The magic comes from each one of us sitting down, having a heartfelt search within ourselves, and having the courage to write down, in order, 12 hallmark ideals that best reflect the traits we aspire most to role model.

But there are no absolutes. For example, some people are readers and masters of the language and some aren't.

Singer and songwriting superstar Joe Cocker is rich from his music. A song he sat down one day and wrote, *"You Are So Beautiful (To Me),"* was voted the most romantic song of the past century.

Upon moving several years ago to a remote rural town of 385 in mountainous central Colorado, Cocker put being a good neighbor at the very top of his Daily Dozen, ahead of furthering his career as a musician. His days as a wild man now long behind him, Cocker reassessed his own core values.

Cocker and his wife Pam formed the charity-driven "Cockers Kids Foundation" and have plowed tremendous amounts of time, energy and money into helping improve the lives of children throughout their adopted and neighboring communities.

Another superstar – a very different type of linguistic craftsman – got rich reciting poetry despite finishing in the bottom 10% of his high school class of nearly 400. In fact, he finished his senior year 376th out of 391 students.

Though not a scholastic valedictorian, he went on to be a pretty good athlete. Who could ever forget this televised exchange between a bombastic chainsmoking reporter and that motormouthed kid from Louisville with the not-so-hot grades?

The reporter was Howard Cosell. The athlete was Muhammad Ali. The two were discussing Ali's brash confidence prior to his 1968 title fight with Zora Folley – the last fight Ali would have before being stripped of his title for refusing induction into the service for religious reasons.   Four-and-a-half years later, Ali would be vindicated in court.

Said Cosell to Ali, "You're sounding rather truculent."

Without batting an eye, Ali looked at Cosell blankly and immediately replied, "Whatever truculent means, if it's *good,* I'm that!"

Ali was a great communicator and brilliant showman – but not much of a grammarian – so Muhammad filled his Daily Dozen with things he felt were more important. In my first book, I wrote about watching Ali, 25 years after that Cosell interview, spend 5½ hours and miss two airplanes by remaining seated in an old, tiny Coral Gables bookstore simply because so many people showed up to see him.

Twice that day Betty Mitchell, Angelo Dundee's long-time administrative assistant, canceled and rescheduled Muhammad's airline reservations from Miami back to Louisville.

When I asked Betty about Ali in the bookstore, she simply said that when Muhammad called, all he said was, "If all these people wanna meet Ali, then Ali wants to meet all these people." Having fully explained, he then hung up the phone.

Ali's 45-minute visit ended up lasting nearly six hours.

So, everyone's list of what belongs on their own personal Daily Dozen is wonderfully unique. To Muhammad, being kind to others is right up near the top – second only to a steadfast and unwavering commitment to his faith.

6 Steps to Creating *YOUR OWN* Daily Dozen

Step #1: **Think. Then think some more. Give the idea deep, quality thought before you write down *anything*.**

Think carefully about the mission at hand. Reflect on what *specific* things you could do to build equity in yourself as a quality person. At this point all you want to do is think about all the different spokes life takes and which ones bring you the most personal pride.

If possible, think about the topic while you exercise. The endorphin release from exercising will serve a dual purpose: First, it'll naturally make you feel better. Second, you'll be in a positive frame of mind to weigh the relative value of other positive thoughts.

If you're not an exerciser, go somewhere quiet – where you can think and not be interrupted.

As you give the topic serious consideration, specific values will begin crystallizing and starting to repeat themselves over and over in your mind. Repetitive thought somehow bubbles the keepers to the surface, separating them from the less-important. Many of your strongest core ideals will separate from the others and simply float to the forefront of your thoughts.

Step #2: **Laundry-list your ideas.**

There are easy-to-use practice pages at the end of this chapter. Once you've given your list careful thought, transcribe what you've brainstormed onto paper and jot down as many ideas as you can think of. Use phrases, buzzwords, sentences, emotions, dreams, ambitions – anything that helps capture the gist of your ideas. Everything is important; there are no right or wrong ideas.

What you want to accomplish here is to transfer the ferris wheel of ideas that are spinning around your head into notes on a page. I had 17 or 18 before I whittled my list down to the final 12.

By laundry-listing, you should have way more than just a dozen ideas. The more you've got to choose from, the better off you are. The eventual dozen will rise to the surface if you treat this exercise like a handwritten truth serum.

Step #3: **Examine, then rate, your entire list.**

Some ideas might be interrelated. If they are, try and summarize them more succinctly to capture the overlapping message. For example, "Staying physically fit" and "Working out regularly" deal with the same issue.

Once you've stratified your brainstorming list, take each item and give it a letter grade on how important (deep-down) it really is to you. Grade the most important "A's", then "B's", then "C's."

Group your ideas according to their relative importance.

Step #4: **Wordsmith each idea carefully.**

Don't cheat yourself here. This is an exercise in precision, not speed. Take the time to select the *exact* combination of words that precisely expresses the specific thought you want to capture. Every word is important so take whatever time is necessary to pinpoint the character trait you aspire to role-model.

Remember to describe each trait in the present tense! These are traits we intend to demonstrate daily, so write them in the present tense.

Step #5: **Preliminarily rank your list.**

Stack rank you're "A's" in numerical order of importance, with #A1 being the most important. Then move onto your "B's," then lastly the "C's." At the end, you'll have a tentative list in order of importance, 1-15, 16, 18 or however many – with that number one (#1) of your "A Group" being the most important personal value of all.

Step #6: **Test the order of your tentative list and either buy it or change it.**

In my case, I shuffled mine around a bit. My tentative first pass at establishing their order was close, but not the way they finally ended up. After additional careful thought, I moved several up and down, then tossed a couple out.

Work diligently on finalizing your list until you are 100-percent certain the final order has each desired trait *exactly* where it belongs and its written description captures the precise ideal the way you want it defined.

When you think you've got it, test yourself by making sure you know the specific reason each of the 12 traits on your list is slotted exactly where it is.

Each of your final 12 will have its proper and appropriate place in your final rankings!

Don't shortchange yourself by not carefully analyzing every trait on its standalone, deserved merit. If it's important enough to write down, it's important enough to carefully contemplate, then accurately rank.

In the end, *you* are the one who's got to buy what's on that final list – plus its ranking order of importance. After all – you wrote it, so you *should* buy it.

Once written, post your list somewhere handy where you can refer to it often. Each time you refer to it – test it. If it's still perfect, then buy the list all over again and do your best to keep living it.

On the following pages are sample worksheets to help develop Your Own Daily Dozen. When you're done – and buy the final result – then transcribe, laminate and post your list somewhere you'll see it often. When summarized, the list can easily fit in your wallet or on the back of a business card.

By creating Your Daily Dozen, you've defined, in writing, the person you want to be. *Who* you want to be has gone from a nebulous, undefined collection of thoughts to a specific contract that specifically shapes you into the person you want others to see.

Take the time to conscientiously complete each list, then pursue its attainment with zealous pride. Your Personal Daily

Dozen will help you live a good and honorable life while your Business Dozen helps define your professional identity.

Having embraced and lived those gratifying dozen important traits, as you get older and pause to look back on the footprints you've left – well, you'll have the great good fortune to enjoy the journey, all over again.

(see chart on next page)

Step #1
"Building Your Daily Dozen"

Step #1: Think carefully. Invest the necessary time to give the concept some deep quality thought before jotting down any notes.

Think through the many facets of life and fulfillment that could help define who you truly want to be. These traits are often things you admire in others.

Remember the "Three Musketeers of Balance": *Physical, Fiscal & Cerebral.* After you've carefully thought things through, brainstorm your notes and thoughts below:

Brainstorming Ideas

A		L	
B		M	
C		N	
D		O	
E		P	
F		Q	
G		R	
H		S	
I		T	
J		U	
K		V	

Step #2

"Building Your Daily Dozen"

Step #2: *Laundry-list your ideas.*

Convert your brainstorming ideas into specific traits that might help shape you into the person (or worker) you'd like to become. At this point, make no judgments on ranking individual points – simply transcribe and jot down all your clarified ideas.

ITEM	PERSONAL TRAITS OF IMPORTANCE
A	
B	
C	
D	
E	
F	
G	
H	
I	
J	
K	
L	
M	
N	
O	
P	
Q	

Step #3

"Building Your Daily Dozen"

Step #3: *Examine your list.*

Scrutinize your Step #2 Laundry List and decide which traits are related and which are not really core-critical to defining who you aspire to be.

Then, sort your traits into three categories – "A," "B," or "C" – with A's being most important, B's in the middle, and C's the least important.

Category A, B, or C?	Reexamined Personal Traits of Importance
A B C	
A B C	
A B C	
A B C	
A B C	
A B C	
A B C	
A B C	
A B C	
A B C	
A B C	
A B C	
A B C	
A B C	
A B C	

Step #4

"Building Your Daily Dozen"

Step #4: *Wordsmithing every idea.*

For each item on your list (starting with your *A's*), redefine and select the precise wording to accurately capture exactly how to best-describe each important idea. Describe everything in the present tense (ex.: *"Manage the Worry Circle daily."*)

Category A, B, or C?			Precise Definition of Personal Traits of Importance
A	*B*	*C*	
A	B	C	
A	B	C	
A	B	C	
A	B	C	
A	B	C	
A	B	C	
A	B	C	
A	B	C	
A	B	C	
A	B	C	
A	B	C	
A	B	C	
A	B	C	
A	B	C	

Step #5
"Building Your Daily Dozen"

Step #5: *Preliminarily rank your list.*

First, stack-rank within your *A's*; then within your *B's*; then within your *C's*. List your *A's*, by importance (starting with #A1 at the top). Your least important *C*-item should be at the bottom.

Ranking: 1-12+	Preliminary Ranking of Personal Traits of Importance
1	
2	
3	
4	
5	
6	
7	
8	
9	
10	
11	
12	
13	
14	
15	
16	
17	

Step #6

"Building Your Daily Dozen"

Step #6: *Test the final order of your list.*

Either buy your list, as is, or change it. When you're done, cut the list to the Top 12. Every trait should have its exact and precise place in the order by the time you're finished.

YOUR Personal Daily Dozen:

Final Ranking	Reexamined *FINAL ORDER*, Personal Traits of Importance
#1	
#2	
#3	
#4	
#5	
#6	
#7	
#8	
#9	
#10	
#11	
#12	

Daily Dozen Chapter Summary

Contracting with yourself to identify and *write down* your core values is an important part of life enhancement. A goal is a dream with a deadline, written on paper. Until you write it, you don't own it.

Your Daily Dozen is *your* dream, written *for* yourself, *about* yourself. All that remains after it's created is for you to do your best to bring it to life.

Your core life values are now summarized by your Daily Dozen. If the list reflects who you want to be, and what you want to stand for, then you have constructed a solid framework for self-improvement. If you live it, you will grow internally rich, regardless of your financial means. All the dollars, Euros, yen, pesos and lira in the world can't buy the inner peace that comes by a life lived to the guidelines set by a well-written Daily Dozen.

Money can buy a lot of things, but not contentment.

Creating a well-written Personal Daily Dozen takes a lot of careful thought and study. It is *not* a five-minute exercise. Your goal is to create a 12-point description using precisely the right words. You want your list to stand the test of time. Your personal list should rarely change, if ever.

Your Business Daily Dozen will be much more dynamic and need to be updated as work and professional responsibilities change from job-to-job and career-to-career. As a rule of thumb, double-check its on-going accuracy at least twice each year.

Create or change every Daily Dozen with care and thoughtfulness. Pretend you're building a boat that won't sink in stormy seas – and that *you* are its sole passenger. A well-constructed boat will last for decades. So will a well-crafted personal Daily Dozen.

Your Daily Dozen is not a press release describing who you already are, but rather a blueprint of improvement for whom you strive to be. Keep it often in sight and – even more often – in mind. That list is your recipe for a Pro Leisure Tour level of internal happiness.

A rock-solid inner peace will blossom from living your plan. Do you have that inner peace? Over time, you can't fool yourself. *You* know the truth and the truth – *the inner truth* – is the ultimate measurement tool by which your progress is measured.

Write it, post it, look at it, own it, and chase it. And take pride in what you've written. Live the life you've signed up to live.

And love the journey it takes you on, too.

Chapter 5

PDs & The Hourglass of Time

Each of us has a finite number of Personal Days (PD's) during our lifetime. PD's are free-choice days unencumbered by work responsibilities. The *Stage of Life* chart on the following page illustrates the declining number of expected days remaining in our lives as we reach five arbitrary life milestones:

1. Our birth. The hourglass flips over here and our time on earth begins.

2. Age 21. When we reach 21, we assume (for the sake of discussion) the beginning of a 40-year working career. Up to this point, the years of our youth are pretty much two decades of Personal Days in advance of four decades of work.

3. Age 45. At 45 we're still probably able to physically do what we'd like to do and have reached a more comfortable level in our earning power. Assuming we started working at 21, the age of 45 means we've ground our way through 60-percent of our working career with 16 years yet remaining.

4. Age 61. The arbitrary age of 61 is when we retire after 40 years of work. From this point forward, our working careers complete, every remaining day of our life is assumed to be a Personal Day.

5. And, finally, at the finish line. American men live an average of 72.3 years, women nearly seven years longer (to 79.1). Some arrive early, some arrive late, but everybody, sooner or later, arrives in the same predicament – permanently horizontal.

At that point, the finish line, the game's over. We leave the scene and all our chips go back into play in life's perpetual global casino.

The chart on the following page charts our expected mortality.

Stage of Life Chart
(Number of Days Remaining)

All the "Remaining Day" numbers below are based on an American's current average life expectancy *(per World Almanac, 2001).*

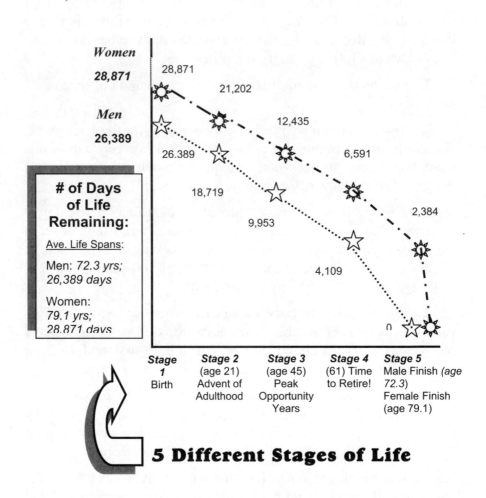

5 Different Stages of Life

Two Important Things to Remember about PD's:

♦ *The Personal Days of our life are front and back-loaded.*

Three-fourths (a full 75%) of our Personal Days occur during our youth and old age. Once we begin our working careers, four decades are chewed up with only 25% of our life's allocation of free time available to do what we'd like to do or achieve what we'd like to achieve.

♦ *Women's totals (above) do not include the extra pressures of maternal and familial commitments.*

Many women have mid-life responsibilities that men don't and these added burdens often *reduce* the true number of Personal Days they have during their lifetimes.

For the sake of continued discussion, let's equate every single day of our life's allocation to individual grains of sand housed inside an hourglass. Once you're born, the hourglass is turned over and the sand begins dropping, grain by daily grain, from your future on the top half of the hourglass to your past on the bottom half.

There are a finite number of grains in the hourglass. Each morning you've got one less up top and one more in the ever-growing glass-enclosed sand dune down below.

If you are a man with an average life expectancy, there are 26,389 grains of sand up top the day you're born. Some lucky men are poured more; many – unfortunately – are poured less. The late comedian George Burns was lucky enough to get 10,000 grains of sand. Perhaps it was a bonus for all the joy he brought so many people for so long.

But for every George Burns with 10,000 extra days, somewhere there's a man who's shorted by the same amount.

The same, obviously, holds true for women. For every Queen Mum of England who lives past 100, there's an unfortunate woman shorted her just due.

Women, on average, live nearly 2,400 more days than men, perhaps as a reward for surrendering so much time during the prime of their lives with maternal and familial responsibilities.

Regardless of how many grains are in the hourglass at the start, every midnight releases one of them from the top-half of the hourglass to the bottom. And gravity has no reverse gear; one the granule's gone, it's gone.

A certain number of those grains of sand in the top of your hourglass – 40 years worth – are allocated to be spent working. So, at any stage of an adult life, only a portion of your given number of grains are allocated for personal use.

Those non-working days are your Personal Days.

And since your Personal Days, unfortunately, are predominantly front and back-loaded toward the beginning and ending stages of your life, Living a Pro Leisure Tour lifestyle helps temper the effects of such an unfair reality.

If you die prematurely, before reaching 61 and prior to finishing your assigned 40 years of work, you're cheated out of Personal Days, not Working Days.

The same holds true if you reach 61 but not the expected male longevity of 72.3 years or female average nearly seven years longer (79.1). Every day you're shortchanged was a Personal Day unfairly deducted from your life's allocation.

(see chart on next page)

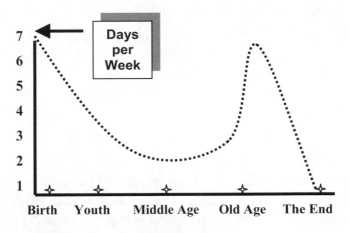

When Your Personal Days Occur
(Throughout Your Lifetime)

The Key Point

The major message is simple: **You must embrace a sense of urgency in living each and every day to the best of your ability.** *If you squeeze as much happiness, fulfillment, and contentment out of every opportunistic sunrise, you will have a better life.*

The inexorable truth for all of us is that our days are numbered and they do, in fact, drop like grains of sand from our future to our past. And those grains honor the laws of gravity. Once dropped, forever lost. None have retrorockets strong enough to boost them back up to the top-half of the hourglass.

The big question – the never-known mystery – is how many grains of sand were poured into each of our hourglasses to begin with. There could be a lot. But then again, maybe not.

Remember a couple other important considerations with PDs. One is factoring in your family life history. Another is the impact of personal habits. If neither points toward longevity, you must accelerate your sense of urgency to achieve what you want during your expected lifetime.

Sometimes a bit of behavior modification helps, too.

Baseball great Mickey Mantle, for example, guessed wrong in that regard. Mick's family died young and he expected to also. So, he drank away his PDs and died prematurely – and a much poorer man for doing so. Mick cheated himself out of a lot of living.

Family history can be a clue. But that's all it is – a clue, not an answer.

In my case, one side of my parental lineage history is long-lived. The other is short-lived. So, knowing that – what does that make me, besides confused? One thing it's helped propel is an accelerated and heightened sense of urgency for living. Simplistically, I added up both parents' life spans, divide by two, and anticipate living the average.

Hopefully I'll last a little longer.

Assume you've been allocated enough sand to get in your shoes and maybe itch a bit in your swimsuit. But never assume you've been given giant mounds to build a sandcastle. If you got that much, then *great* – you got a bonus. But live every day like it's a bonus grain of sand and you'll be richly rewarded throughout your lifetime.

The following chart breaks down for men and women our average daily life allocations into Total Days, Working Days and Personal Days.

At a glance, you'll be able to see – in finite numbers – just how important it is to be grateful for each day you've been given.

As you look at the chart, think about what's important to you. How well are you living your priorities? If family's first, then how do *you* spend your free time? With them? Or buried in chores and/or personal pursuits? Reality checks are always good, never bad, so make sure to give yourself one from time to time.

It's also good to compare your goals crafted by your Daily Dozen with the average amount of sand in the hourglass you might have remaining to get them all completed. The older you get, the narrower the window is open.

The next two pages contain charts. The first takes a look at how many "Total Days" we're expected to live, and how many remain as we pass through different milestones of life.

The second page contains a chart detailing how many Personal Days we've got during an average lifetime. It, too, peels our total number of Personal Days apart (life stage by life stage) to illustrate how many we have as we pass through life's series of birthday cakes, each impaled with one more candle than the year before.

Our Personal Days are, clearly, front-end and back-end loaded to the beginning and ending stages of life. The Personal Day chart is a quantified, stark reminder that the number we have is finite. At a glance, you'll see there aren't many – and certainly never enough.

None, of course, should be wasted.

(see charts on next two pages)

How Many Personal Days Do *You* Have Left?

	Life Allocation Chart	Men	Women
Average Life in Years	Average Life Span	72.3 years	79.1 years
Ave. Life in Total # of Days	*Total Allocation of Days in Lifetime (including Leap Years)*	*26,389*	*28,871*
At Age 21	(Life Days already used at 21)	(7,670)	(7,670)
	Life Days remaining at age 21	18,719	21,201
	(Less Work Days remaining)	(10,435)	(10,435)
	Net Personal Days Remaining	***8,284***	***10,766***
At Age 45	(Life Days already used at 45)	(16,436)	(16,436)
	Days Remaining at age 45	9,953	12,435
	(Less Work Days Remaining)	(4,174)	(4,174)
	Net Personal Days Remaining	***5,779***	***8,261***
At Age 61	(Life Days already used at 61)	(22,280)	(22,280)
	Days Remaining at age 61	4,109	6,591
	Less Work Days Remaining	0	0
	Net Personal Days Remaining	***4,109***	***6,591***
At 72.3	Less Days Used at age 72.3	26,389	26,389
	Days Remaining at age 72.3	0	2,482
	Less Work Days Remaining	0	0
	Net Personal Days Remaining	***0***	***2,482***

When Your Personal Days Occur

Stage:	# of Personal Days	Men	Women
Birth to 21	Net # of Personal Days, age 0-21	7,620	7,620
21 to 45	Net # of Personal Days, age 21-45 *(primarily vacation & weekends)*	2,505	2,505
45 to 61	Net # of Personal Days, age 45-61 *(primarily vacation & weekends)*	1,670	1,670
61 to 72.3	Net # of Personal Days, age 61-72.3	4,109	4,109
Women beyond 72.3	Net # of Personal Days, age 72.3– 79.1	0	2,482
Lifetime Perspective	*Total # of Personal Days During Entire Expected Lifetime*	*15,904*	*18,386*
Lifetime	# of full <u>years</u>' worth of Personal Days	43.5 full years	50.3 full years
% of early & late-in-life days	Youth and Old Age stages combined *(as a % of Life's Total # of PD's)*	73.7%	63.6%
# of PD's while working	*# of Personal Days spread out during our 40-year working career*	4,175	4,175
% of life's PD's while working	*% of Life's Personal Days that occur during an average 40-year working career:*	**26.3%**	**22.7%**

It's *startling* to note *(above)* that during the prime 40-years of our expected lifetime, we'll only have the opportunity to enjoy *one-fourth* of our hoped-for allocation of Personal Days!

Personal Days should be cherished, not wasted. Do your best to never squander a single one.

A quick study of the breakdown of Personal Days in your life is probably a bit of a surprise. And it should be.

♦ ***Three-fourths (75%!) of ALL the personal days in your life take place during your youth and old age!*** *Only 25% of our personal days come during a prime 40-year period that spans the heart of adulthood.*

♦ ***That 25% translates into a mere 4,175 Personal Days occurring during the entire <u>4-decade</u> span of our prime 40-year working career!***

With such a small number of personal choice days to begin with (less than 11½ total years of our entire projected lifetime), it's clear that *everyone* should live the prime of their life with a heightened sense of respect and urgency in order to achieve their most important personal goals.

This urgency is extra-important for women. By bearing the brunt of running the home and the often overwhelming maternal obligations of child-rearing, the days in the chart that are called PD's often are anything *but*!

Family life during the child-rearing years has a *far greater* compression factor on available Personal Days for women than men and those additional demands and pressures also serve to underscore the vital need to protect every true Personal Day.

Your Four Choices

Male *or* female, with such a modest number of Personal Days, it's more important that ever to decide right now how you're going to utilize each one. You've got four choices. You can either: *Cherish* them; *Invest* them; *Spend* them; or *Waste* them.

Live each PD by whatever means brings you the most happiness. But remember: When it comes to Personal Days, there are no "do-overs" or "mulligans." Time is irreplaceable, which is why it's more important than money. Money comes and goes.

Time simply goes. Once the sand granule drops, it sits motionless for eternity. It's gone, for good.

Bullfroggin' & Rock Hoppin' thru Life

Once we decide *how* we want to utilize our time (Cherish, Invest, Spend or Waste it) the next important skill is to learn how to get more done – preferably as well and as quickly as possible. In order to maximize our achievements with the minimum amount of wasted time, we need to learn how to quickly develop strategic plans for improving life at home, and in the office.

That learned skill is the ability to *"See the End & Work Backward."* All high performers first clearly define the goals they plan on reaching, then road-map a plan backward from their end goal to *exactly* where they presently stand.

Then they execute that plan flawlessly. We will learn that valuable life skill in a later chapter (Chapter 12). That skill – learning how to smartly work in straight lines – is another one of those helpful things that college really ought to teach but doesn't. Learning to quickly develop strategic plans is an ultra-valuable life skill transferable to both business situations and life-at-home challenges.

Venturing from where we currently are to Life on the Pro Leisure Tour is much like stepping across a succession of dry rocks sticking above the surface of a wide, flowing river. By taking one careful, confident step at a time we can all cross the river fairly quickly without falling in.

Early in the book, we learned what to worry about and what not to. Learning to manage *The Worry Circle* was like stepping off the riverbank and hopping onto our first safe, dry stepping-stone.

Deciding and writing down our Daily Dozen – defining *who* exactly we aspired to be – was taking a measured hop forward to the next.

Feeling a finite and heightening sense of urgency in the ways and whys of how to use our time – maximizing our life's unknown allocation of PD's – is yet another.

We're now nearly halfway across the gurgling river and our shoes are still dry. The plan is for those shoes to remain that way when we arrive on the far bank of the PLT.

Our next midstream boulder-hop deals with job satisfaction – when to switch jobs and when to stay put. Enjoying what we do is very important and in the following dozen or so pages we'll dissect when the time is right to stay and when it's time to move on to new challenges.

From there we'll hop past midstream and examine the specific traits of high performers – what makes them flourish at what they do – and then rate ourselves to see how we compare.

At that point, we're well over halfway to life on the Pro Leisure Tour. Step by measured step, we'll get *exactly* where we want to go.

Chapter 6

When to Switch Jobs

I include this chapter because a lot of friends and business contacts call or write when they seem to be bottled or throttled in their existing line of work. I'm not an executive recruiter or job search expert. Never have been. Never profess to be.

But the topic – changing jobs – ties in beautifully to Living Life on the Pro Leisure Tour. After all, if you don't enjoy what you do for a living, chances are it'll be pretty tough to be content.

Over the years I've seen some smart people make dumb career decisions and not-as-bright ones make fortunes. I always get a kick out of watching someone chase a dream and tackle it around the waist. How can you not root for someone to succeed when they know what they really want to do in life?

And to me, that seems to be the hard part – knowing just what it is in life you really want to do.

Close to home, my father never found himself a fulfilling career. Part of it, my mother always thought, was that his entire adult life he never really figured out what it was he wanted to do.

He had jobs, sure. My dad ground out a modest living selling hoists, forklift trucks and materials handling equipment for Yale & Towne. Then Yale was bought out by Eaton Corporation and things all changed. Eventually he was surplused due to a reorganization.

My father faced the news with the doom of the condemned. For all intents and purposes, his life's identity crumbled to dust the day he was jettisoned with a severance package at the age of 53.

In my father's mind, he was suddenly an unemployable old man. He was beaten. He lost the ability to look at the world through the eyes of a child. My father lived another decade and died from cancer at 63. He didn't have much fun during his final decade. His less-than-fulfilling business career sapped his zest for living.

I frequently read that the average American worker has seven jobs and five separate careers during her or his adult lifetime. Job-hopping is more common now than a couple decades ago. It has to be. The life cycle of organizations seems much shorter and as companies evolve in different directions like an amoeba randomly crawling across a microscope slide, different required skill sets come and go.

Keeping your skills fresh – and competitive – is now almost *required*, regardless what you do for a living. With an ever-dynamic marketplace in an expanding and contracting economy, workers can either voluntarily seek out new knowledge and skills or forcefully try to digest them when cascaded down as necessary from employers.

Like so many things we've already talked about, it's far better to invest knowledge equity in yourself pro-actively than reactively.

During a strong economy, growing your personal equity translates into increased job opportunities and more money. In a shrinking economy, the most valuable workers are always the last to go. So, as times get tough, "continuous skill improvement" can translate into a three-word synonym for "job security."

The impact of the ever-evolving digital revolution has been like watching a real-life video game. I worked for a couple years in Silicon Valley and told people that "408" (the area code) was nothing more than adult Disneyland. It was amazing to watch geniuses living in station wagons waiting for a million-dollar score that rarely ever came.

Most of us don't have either the gumption or vehicle to do such a thing so we live more normally and opt instead to change jobs from time-to-time.

From what I've observed, there are right ways and wrong ways to make a career move. Keep these next few tips in mind as you go through the process of self-assessing where you are in your life and career. Hopefully, you're where you want to be. If not, this chapter should help.

Remember: Living Life on the Pro Leisure Tour means you've got to be happy with the circumstances of your life situation. *What you do for a living, obviously, is a key part of the formula.*

Job-changing is always stressful. We all know that. But everybody was always looking for a job when they found the one they're currently in, so the looking stress isn't really worth burning energy over. You've done it before and succeeded. You'll succeed again. So why worry yourself into a spiral of angst?

Remember what we said earlier about what in life we choose to worry about: Worry only about what *you* can control. And in the context of looking for a new opportunity, you *can* control what you look for, how diligently and smartly you're looking, and how well-prepared you are when you interview.

You can also control your appearance, your attitude, and how aggressively you decide to pursue something you really want to do.

When you positively and methodically apply all those things, you will succeed.

Plus, we know endorphins are our secret weapons. Exercise before an interview and chances are you'll interview better. Why? You'll feel better, sharper, and internally more confident. Beautifully, you can control those things.

So, the fear of looking is really nothing to fear at all provided you commit to controlling the things you properly should.

Where is job-switching on the list of life's biggest stresses?

It's a relative stress. At times it looms large and can totally dominate the circular rubber walls of your Worry Circle.

But compared to the loss of child, spouse, medical emergency or unhappy divorce, it's so far down on the totem pole you'd have to dig deep to find it.

A Memorable Piece of Great Advice

One of the best pieces of advice on job-changing I've ever heard came to me from my good friend George Simmons. George was the long-time head of the sales training school at Xerox's international training facility.

For nearly 30 years, George was very picky about who he hired to come in to teach – he believed it took a very specific set of skills and personal attributes – but once selected, each instructor became a lifelong protégé. George was a mentor to many, long before mentoring became a popular thing to do.

George saw some tremendous talents come and go. Some rose the ladder of responsibility to great wealth and others left the company and found huge success in other organizations.

He also saw some great talents leave and fall flat on their face. Over time, George developed a brief but cagey opinion on when to stay and when to go.

"Always ask yourself two questions," George would say earnestly. "Do you enjoy what you're doing and are you making any money?"

George didn't believe in overcomplicating things that required no complication. He also believed job-fulfillment was easy to dissect and had its measure boiled down to those two very simple questions.

Concerning the answers to his two questions, George was, again, succinct. "If the answers are *yes* and *yes*," he'd say, "then stay put.

"If the answers are one *yes* and one *no*, then try and fix the *no*. Try and figure out how to make the job more enjoyable, more fulfilling, or try and figure out how to make more money doing what you're doing since you enjoy the work.

"If you can't change either, then you simply have to decide whether the *yes* outweighs the *no*. And if it does, then sign up for it and don't complain." Since career doors are never locked, George had a very short fuse for whiners.

But George had a different response if your two answers were both *"no."*

"If both are *no's*, then it's time to move on. If you don't like what you're doing and aren't making any money, then it's time to go.

"The sooner the better," he added. "Life's too short to waste it."

Dealing with Job Frustration

Everybody gets frustrated. No news there. Frustration is a huge job-change catalyst. Sometimes those frustrations come from all the masks everyone in the office or organization is wearing.

Masks are invisible disguises that are part of every worker and company. At work, the mask disguises you as the person you want to appear to be to others. Not who you really *are* necessarily, but who you pretend to be.

Masks can come in a myriad of forms: Clothing selections, hairstyle regulations, acceptable expressions, and grooming rules, for example. Words can be a mask. If you ever sat in on a long corporate meeting with a brand new #2 lead pencil and ticked off the number of buzzwords you heard, that new pencil would emerge from the meeting the perfect size to keep score at miniature golf.

Large corporations, often by necessity, can be the worst mask-issuing offenders and often host what seem like perpetual costume balls. In extreme cases a company can go overboard and employees don blinking neon masks of overt political correctness and circular doublespeak. Worker individualism is often repressed and decision-making is restricted to a relative few.

To some extent, companies sort of *need* to issue masks, since they help create, shape, and maintain its corporate or organizational identity.

In big corporations, a carefully crafted disguise is part of the team uniform. Mission statements help define the role each employee is expected to play. The disguise – sometimes multi-layered – is what employees are asked to wear in public. They are usually expected to wear it internally, too.

Companies have the right – a very expensive and hard-earned right – to make you wear masks. In addition to your specific job responsibilities, role-modeling the proper corporate identity is something else you are paid to do.

For individuals, these disguises are often easy to wear quite comfortably since rejection kicks back the mask, not the wearer underneath. The mask separates the inner you – the real you – from the person performing the work. You wear the mask because you *have* to – and not because you really *want* to.

Unmasking is hard. Unmasked, we are about as vulnerable as we'll ever be. If you are unmasked – and rejected – then it's *the real you* whose ego is taking the shot.

Life is more fulfilling if you have the courage to consciously remove those disguises – every single layer – from time-to-time and just toss them in the trash. Life's better, but harder, without them.

When you're chasing a *passion*, you rarely even bother with a mask. When you're working at a *job*, you always do.

For some, it's much easier to *say* "remove it" than it is to actually do it. Removing masks can be a terrifying experience for a person who's lived their entire adult life hidden behind them. To them, a mask is as taken for granted as an attached limb.

When the mask your job forces you to wear is too tough to look at in the mirror any more, then chances are it's time for a change. But remember: Every *job* comes with its own new costume wardrobe. Expect that if you decide to switch employers.

Pursuing a *passion* is a different story. People pursue passions far more lightly-cloaked than people reporting for duty in the salt mines.

To this day, George's advice on when to switch jobs has remained rock-solid.

I'll also add one other quick point: You're always better off leaving one year too soon than staying one year too long. And if you're head's not quite sure it's time to go, well, your stomach usually is.

"The human brain can rationalize anything," said Virginia investment research specialist Chip Ford. "Learn to make the big decisions above the waist and below the neck."

Put simply, when it's time to go – it's time to go. Trust your gut and follow through in a quality way. The vision of your future is before you. Pausing to look over your shoulder and grumble about yesterday's news wastes time and energy you could've more smartly used to take another step forward.

Another important consideration in seeking new opportunities is understanding specifically *why* you want to change. Leaving because of a manager is not usually a good reason.

Try not to leave a job because of the boss or stay in a job because of the boss. Bosses change. Good ones move up or on. Bad ones move out. Focus on the job and its possibilities – <u>not</u> the boss.

Managing a boss is its own matador-like art form. Many good books have been written on the subject. Consult one for suggestions if you find yourself wrestling with the need to do so.

But if (and when) you do decide to leave one job for another: *Always* leave on a positive note. Always take the high road and burn no bridges.

A decade ago an acquaintance locked herself in an office, got on the corporate P.A. and cussed everybody out over the loudspeaker for about 10 minutes before she finally ran out of steam. She was then escorted out the building, never to return. By purging her frustrations, she ruined 15 loyal years of service and verbally firebombed her own bridge.   Returning was now impossible, as was getting a quality referral.

Venting serves no positive purpose, so resist the urge. Remember: *Take the high road. The low road's too crowded.* Self-torching the cloth of your own career destroys any future chance of parlaying that business portion of your life into anything positive in a similar industry.

During my 20 years in high-level selling, training, and talent development, I've seen literally hundreds of marketing talents come and go.

Some flourished after they left.   A few skyrocketed into the high-performance stratosphere.

Some, however, withered.

I believe there is a reason, a very simple reason, they failed to flourish: People who leave a job, generally speaking, are doing so for one of two reasons: They're either running *from* something or running *to* something.

There is a <u>massive</u> and <u>monumental</u> difference between the two.

People who exit hastily because they're running *from* something rarely succeed in their next job.   I've met some world class athletes and been to the Olympic Games, but I've never met anyone yet who's fast enough to outrun their problems.

You just can't do it.

Kenny Tennant, a long-time friend and well-known telecommunications recruiter based in Atlanta, has repeatedly mentioned that whenever someone leaves a long-tenured job, they are more likely to flourish in their second future position than the first.

Paraphrasing Kenny, there are simply too many bitter toxins and ingrained habits to flush from the system the first time. The first job after leaving a long-tenured job is the "purge-and-deprogram" job.   The second job is the flourish job.   By then, workers have figured out what makes them happy and end up in better-fitting environments.

So, running *from* something *to* just another job will probably not be fulfilling. But running *to* something you'll really enjoy – a passion – probably will.

Top-notch New York-based executive recruiter Corey Roberts subscribes wholeheartedly to the critical matching of skill sets and personalities to specific corporate cultures.

"Every company has its own culture," Roberts said. "Above all, I try to match the culture of the candidate with the culture of the company. If the company knows what it's trying to achieve with the hiring – and the candidate is qualified and a good fit for the environment – the candidate will do an excellent job. He or she will flourish.

"Everybody wins," he added. "That's the most rewarding part of the job – matching talented people with great opportunities to solve problems for companies that need them."

Roberts believes there are magnetic pulls of differing strengths between every candidate and every corporate culture. Sometimes the two magnets strongly attract; sometimes they repel. Sometimes there's only a weak or moderate attraction. What Roberts seeks is a maximum-strength match. He prefers working with women and men who are clearly focused on running *toward* a new challenge – not running *from* an old one.

Knowing that running *from* anything rarely has any long-term benefits, carefully examine what type of job or career option you'd really enjoy performing. If you don't really know, every library and bookstore carries books that help you figure it out. Read through a couple if it's time for a change but you're not exactly sure what you'd really like to do.

You can also turn to the Internet for research, ideas and information. Pool whatever resources you need to – especially friends, confidants, and respected business connections – to learn as much as you can about directions you may be interested in pursuing.

For many people, it's easier to know what they _don't_ want than it is to figure out what type of work they'd really enjoy doing. Too many people equate dream job happiness with relative poverty. Too many believe that what they really want to do in life won't enable them to earn a good living.

That need not be the case. But since they feel that way, what do they end up doing?

They do nothing. They sit and ruefully dream – trapped in a *"Can't Because"* web of uncertainty, rather than leaping out of a comfort zone and into something new with a revitalizing and refreshing *"How Can I?"* attitude.

"The key ingredient in a good career change is passion," Chip Ford commented. "Do something you have a passion for. The money will follow if it (money) is important to you."

Running *toward* something will jump-start your working life. When you are running toward something you really want to do – or at least dream of trying – can you take a guess what runs right alongside you?

Right! Endorphins and adrenaline!

Consciously or unconsciously, running *toward* something integrates some passion into a key phase of your life where it was previously missing. Everything gets easier, including tangible, important things like bouncing out of bed in the morning, accomplishing more each day, staying self-motivated to maintain your appearance, and being upbeat, positive and nice to others. Snarling disappears and a bushel basket of goodness ensues.

It's very much a virtuous circle. If you like yourself more, others will like you more, too.

Life gets better, quickly.

"Motivating" vs. "Manipulating"

Most folks happily thrive in people-oriented, highly-motivating environments. People are sad and rarely achieve long-term high-performance in manipulative ones. Both generalizations tend to hold quite true in business as well as personal relationships.

It's important to understand the difference between motivating and manipulating. You need to be able to recognize both. Motivation requires a "win/win" type of commitment while pursuing goals that are good for all. High achievement, high-morale partnerships are necessary to forge strong alliances committed to joint success.

Creating a motivating environment means creating surroundings where people will *want* to do something as opposed to being *directed* to. Self-motivating businesses, organizations, and families are always positioned for long-term success as opposed to shorter-term tactical achievements. Self-motivated people tend to be achievers.

Manipulation, meanwhile, is simply persuading someone to do something that's in the best interest of the persuader and not necessarily anyone else. Rather than forging or welding a joint "win/win" commitment for team success, a manipulator cares only about his or her own particular well-being.

Selfishness is a saboteur.

Few can thrive in a manipulative environment. It's tolerable in the short-term, especially if the financial rewards assuage the misery.

But in the long term, you'd have far more fun playing volleyball in Antarctica.

In summary, I'll echo the succinct words of a trusted friend I worked with for a very long time: "Your heart and soul are a good compass."

In her view, when it was time to go – it was time to go. In many instances, simply by asking the question you provide your own answer. Deep down, she said, you'd know if it were time to

107

leave. In my personal experience, I admire her wisdom. The best career and job changes often come from that valuable zone hidden behind your navel and not the precarious teeter-totter between the ears.

Know what you want to be. Or need to be. Or dream of being. Think forward to that fateful day when your own obituary is printed in the newspaper. What do you want it to say?

Will it report that you did what you always wanted to do? Or will it report you died frustrated because you always wanted to do something else but *"Can't Becaused"* yourself into never bothering to try?

Don't leave obit writing to anyone else. *You* are your own best author.

When you're ready to make a move, reality-test your plans and dreams with a trusted associate. Bare your soul a bit. Bounce your thoughts freely for validation, suggestions and improvement ideas. Encouragement from a trusted source is a startlingly powerful resource.

Like my late father, too many people live a life without ever really knowing what it is they'd really like to do. Even sadder are those who *do* figure it out but lack the courage to try – the *"Can't-Becausers."*

I believe the greatest gift a parent can give a son or daughter is the unconditional support that enables and encourages the child to become the very best they can be at whatever in life they passionately choose to pursue.

In return, the best gift a child can ever give back to a parent is their absolute best effort at whatever dreams they've chosen to chase.

When you merge unconditional support with unbridled effort, you create a motivating environment tailor-made for success.

In 57 of every 100 American families, both parents work. Knowing how to position yourself in a job where you'll thrive brings additive joy to the family unit. The same holds true to help minimize the extra stresses within the already difficult burdens of a single-parent family.

Never, *ever* forget – whether you stay in your current position forever or soon decide to make a change – if you're not learning, you're not growing. And if your kids aren't learning – even as adults – they aren't growing either.

If you work, George Simmons suggests updating your resume twice a year. Every six months you need to objectively step back and look at what you've done – or haven't done – to keep growing. If you've done nothing, then what are you going to do about it?

The same checkpoint holds value for those who pursue personal interests instead of work responsibilities. What have you learned over the past six months that's continued to build equity in yourself en route to attaining maximum achievement for all 12 of your personal Daily Dozen goals?

Bloom where you are planted. But if you're getting no sunshine or water, get yourself transplanted! The quicker you do so, the quicker you'll thrive. And that topic – <u>*thriving*</u> – is precisely what we talk about in the very next chapter.

Life is unquestionably better when you are thriving at home and in the office. The next chapter takes a peek at how to do just that.

Chapter 7

Thrivers, Survivors
&
Chevrolet Drivers

Many years ago I spent an intense 10 months or so working with a dozen experienced sales talents week-after-revolving-door-week. Every Monday brought a new batch.

After three months, it seemed that all the people fell into one of three performance categories. For lack of a better descriptive term, I called them *"Thrivers," "Survivors,"* and *"Chevrolet Drivers."*

It was a catchy phrase that served to slot seemingly everyone who passed through my doors.

Thrivers were the people who made things happen, got things done, and consistently delivered quality, overachieving results. Winning mattered. Prideful and often big-ego'd, *Thrivers* <u>expected</u> to perform at high levels and consistently did.

Survivors were at the other end of the spectrum. Survivors were the low producers, grinding along without drive or ambition. Survivors were minimalists who rarely cared about much of anything. In a company, they are the lowly-valued "LIFO's" – Last In, First Out.

The third group, the *Chevrolet Drivers,* constituted the big high-arching majority segment of the company's human bell curve. Drivers were good, loyal people who did what they're told, usually without complaint, and loyally supported the ambitions of the company. While *Drivers* consistently outperformed *Survivors,* for some reason they were usually less-driven or less-productive than the top-performing *Thrivers.*

A Typically Performing Organization

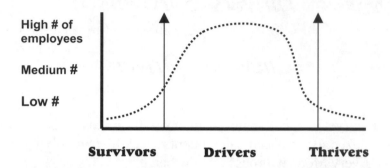

A _Thriving_ Organization

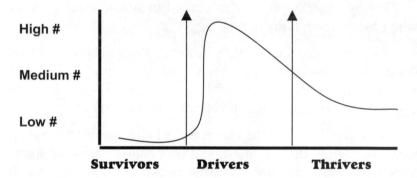

To use a space launch analogy, _Thrivers_ are the rocket engine and _Survivors_ are the exhaust. The _Drivers_ constitute the entire rest of the rocket.

So, looking at the charts above, where would **you** place yourself in your company's graph?

Where would your boss place you?

Where would your most recent performance appraisal place you?

How about at home? And out in the community? If you aren't as far to the right of the graph as you'd like, commit yourself to getting there soon – preferably as soon as possible.

Over time, the existence of these three performance groups – the *Thrivers, Survivors,* and *Drivers* – seemed amazingly consistent, so I took an active interest in trying to figure out why.

I also dropped the "Chevrolet" out of the mid-range "Drivers" description when one of Xerox's top national performers pointed out that she drove a Chevy, by choice, and loved it.

Undaunted and armed with the learnings of countless interviews, post-training follow-ups, field visits, conference calls and roundtable discussions, I developed a "Success Predictability Chart" based on the demonstrated talents of each performer.

In other words, I found it somewhat easy to predict the performance level each person would attain. Accurate self-assessment and employee-assessment are obviously valuable tools for continuous improvement – both personal *and* organizational. The magic then, was figuring out how to move the arrows marking the talent pool as far toward the left axis as possible – thereby decreasing the number of *Survivors* while increasing to a maximum level the number of high-performing *Thrivers.*

Every organization needs both *Thrivers* and *Drivers.* There is an old business adage called the 80/20 rule: 80% of a company's revenues come from a mere 20% of their customers.

Thrivers and *Drivers* are traditionally chartered with protecting, nurturing and growing those precious 80/20 revenue streams. Those revenues are the lifeblood of any successful organization. But how strong a company grows depends on how much heavy lifting those two groups, the *Thrivers* and *Drivers*, can do.

As they go, so goes the company.

Survivors, however, aren't so lucky. In business, *Survivors* are generic and easily replaceable. A lot of organizations have

113

them, but no organization needs them. *Survivors* are disposable employees with no strategic value. When times toughen, they're always the first to go.

A chart of character traits for each of the three performance types is shown on the next page. Take a spoonful of truth serum and see how you stack up.

(see next page)

"Thrivers, Survivors & Drivers"

How Do *YOU* Stack Up?

Personal Traits	"Thrivers"	"Drivers"	"Survivors"
Interest in Learning?	Inquisitive & Proactive	Usually reactive	Minimalists
When Things Happen	*Make* things happen	*React* to what happened	*Wonder* what happened
Endorphin-seeking?	High	Situational	Low
Busy vs. Productive	Productive	Busy	Minimalist
Is a Risk Taker?	Calculated	Modest	Nearly never
Is a Self-starter?	Almost always	Situational	Rarely
Has Balance in Life?	Usually	Sometimes	Rarely
Physically Fit?	Usually	Often	Depends on individual
Adaptable to Change?	Readily	Adjusts	Prefers to fight it
Footprints or Buttprints?	Leaves footprints	Leaves some of both	Leaves buttprints
Role Model & Mentor at Home & in the Community?	Often at home; often in community	Often at home; often in community	Sometimes at home; rarely in community
Lives and Acts with a Sense of Urgency?	Usually	Sometimes	Rarely

"Thrivers, Survivors & Drivers" Professional Traits:

How Do *YOU* Stack Up in the Office?

Business Traits	"Thrivers"	"Drivers"	"Survivors"
Openness to Change	Analytically acceptant quickly	Obedient soldiers	Every change is stupid
Provides Service to Others	Understands importance	Understands importance	Only when required
Energy Level	High	Moderate	Low
Work Discipline	High	Medium	Slothlike; sluglike; comatose or Low
Leadership Skills	Lead	Follow	Often just complain
Value to the Organization	High & critical	Medium & important	Very low & generic
Image in the Office	High	Medium	Low
Loves What They Do	Often	Sometimes	Rarely
Role Model & Mentor?	Often at work	Sometimes at work	Very rarely at work
Fear of Failure	Low	"CYA" mentality	Rarely cares
Works with a Sense of Urgency	Usually	Sometimes	Rarely

Thrivers consistently demonstrate high-performance attributes. Winning matters, as does working in a consistent, high-quality fashion.

By charting the different characteristics of the three performance types, we have – at a glance – a snapshot of key behavioral differences between people who generally achieve more in their business and personal lives than others.

"Thrivers"

What They Are & How to Become One

Thrivers are leaders. They are sorcerers. Rainmakers.

Thrivers make things happen by executing specific plans with an end-goal clearly in mind. Risks are clearly identified and carefully weighed. Thrivers make decisions and don't suffer from paralysis by analysis. They learn from mistakes but don't get hung up on having made them. They constantly move forward.

Thrivers are made more often than born. They capitalize on three things – Knowledge, Skills & Attributes – to consistently achieve what they want to in life. All three topics ("KSA's") are dissected and discussed in clear detail throughout our very next chapter.

In practice, highly successful people don't put a label on everything they do. To a Thriver, life is a series of integrated activities – not identified as "work" or "play." Two consummate American examples are Martha Stewart and Tiger Woods.

Martha Stewart: Thriver Extraoridinaire

It's a long way from making deviled eggs to Wall Street, but Martha Stewart has made the trip in both directions. Her skill at understanding the challenges of all things related to homemaking has made her a household word far beyond the boundaries of the United States.

America's smiling wizard of comfortable living knows everything – and yet never seems to panic, sweat or get dirty. Her success tools – incredible drive, vision, business acumen and work ethic – are all wrapped up in one happy, arms-folded, smiling, confident, pet-loving picture.

Her international company, Martha Stewart Living Omnimedia, Inc., is traded on Wall Street. She is everywhere that media dispenses access to information: Newspapers, radio, television, magazines – you name it, Martha's in it, on it, or making money from it.

Her name is also on nearly *4,000* different products, sold through key partnerships with some of the world's most powerful retailers. The products are developed in complementary concert with the blizzard of helpful how-to advice she dispenses on every conceivable topic through every conceivable distribution channel and an ever-growing number of shrewd strategic alliances.

Martha Kostyra was one of six kids to Polish parents raised in Nutley, New Jersey. Her mother taught Martha most things indoors. Her father, a pharmaceutical salesman, taught her gardening when Martha was just three years old.

Martha worked her way through college as a model and then shifted to Wall Street. There she became a stockbroker and learned to sell in the shadow of the world's busiest trading center.

In 1972, after moving to Westport, Connecticut, Martha traded Wall Street and selling stocks for a catering business. She quickly earned a top-shelf reputation for entertaining with a flair.

Ten full years later, Martha wrote her first book, titled – appropriately enough –*"Entertaining."* The book has sold over 500,000 copies, is in its 30th printing and considered to be pretty much a definitive reference text on the subject.

Recently, Martha aggressively re-channeled her vast talents into building a powerhouse of a business on her name and reputation. She pinpointed an all-consuming focus on the "how-to" market of content and content-driven products for homemakers. Her company is now listed on the New York Stock Exchange – back on Wall Street – and has a very impressive track record.

Martha and her management team focus on eight specific core business segments: Home, Cooking & Entertaining, Gardening, Crafts, Holidays, Baby, Keeping, and Weddings. Each market is driven two ways:

♦ To teach "how to" to as many people as possible through as many communication channels as possible across as much of the world as possible;

♦ And, turning those same consumers into "doers" rather than just readers, listeners, or watchers by offering as many interrelated packages of information, products and services as possible – so they, too, can do things for themselves "the Martha Stewart Way."

How's she doing? Well, Martha's doing quite nicely. Some might say brilliantly. Her business is growing nearly 30% a year and one of her key strategies – Internet commerce – exploded from $5 million in sales to $50 million in just three years. All four of her principal revenue streams – Publishing, Television, Merchandising, and Internet Direct Commerce – are growing.

There's little to indicate this dynamic visionary won't continue to build an extraordinary company that thrives in a swift, decisive, and quality way.

Martha's been named on just about every list of influential leaders published in America. Twice named one of the "50 Most Powerful Women" by Fortune Magazine (1998 & '99), Martha was tabbed one of "America's 25 Most Influential People" by Time Magazine (June 1996). Ms. Stewart's entrepreneurial vision was saluted in October, 2000 when Vanity Fair selected Martha #42 in its annual New Establishment list of the Top 50 Leaders of the Information Age.

The woman has it all, including something hard to teach: *Vision*. Clearly, Martha can see the end – and work backward – with extraordinary effectiveness while quickly circumventing any barriers to performance she might run into.

Martha Stewart lives and works with a persistent sense of energy and urgency and her hard-earned tremendous success validates the pay-off.

Martha is, by every standard, a penultimate Thriver.

Thrivers are always open to better ways of doing things. They seek quality shortcuts – and their successes keep refueling their self-motivation, energy levels, and the reinforced value of staying on the lookout for new tricks to incorporate into their work or living habits.

Thrivers are difficult to replace in any business, community, organization or family unit. Consciously or unconsciously, they are role models for others who admire their ability to get things done and consistently deliver quality results.

Rick Richmond, a very successful real estate developer in Scottsdale, Arizona, points out one of the subtle but very key differences between a Thriver and someone who simply aspires to be one.

"In order to be successful," Richmond says, "you have to know the difference between being busy and being productive. The world is full of busy people. But the number who are productive is much, much less. Busy people stay busy. But productive people get results."

Thrivers enjoy what they do and autograph their work. They are also smart enough to realize that while people might not know how long it took them to do something, those very same people most definitely will know *how well* it was done.

To a Thriver, the "how you do it" is just as important as the "what you do." Thrivers tend to be aware of and heed the advice of a sage old adage: "We tend to judge ourselves by our *intentions* … but others judge us by our *actions*."

Why Tiger Thrives

Golf superstar Tiger Woods is another great example.

Pro golf a shut-up-and-play business. That's the beauty of it. No game, no dough. Big game, big dough. Best-ever game, most-ever dough. If others judge us by our actions, then it's no wonder Tiger is such a tough act for the others on Tour to follow.

Tiger, quite frankly, will continue to get better. The reason is simple – he wants to. And expects to. And if you haven't figured it out by now, when Tiger Woods sets his mind to doing something, generally speaking, it gets done. He *expects* success. He *thrives* on success.

When Tiger first turned professional and Nike boldly signed him to a contract that guaranteed lifetime financial security before he even won a pro tournament, a lot of folks – and count me among them – thought it was "found money." Found money is money given, not earned.

There were pro-Tiger and anti-Tiger forces back then, about evenly split in number. The anti-Tiger movement came about for a couple reasons, not even counting the rednecked racial nonsense.

One reason people didn't like Tiger was that some folks resent "found money" for athletes, especially when it's millions of wrapped and stacked bucks silver-plattered to unproved golfers. After all, golf is hardly the most taxing of pursuits. It's not like boxing, where after a bad night you wake up in a hospital with two puffy eyes and three teeth in a souvenir cup.

In golf, if you have a bad day your pants are still neatly pressed at the end of the round, your hair's still combed and you might just skip Sportscenter that evening to sulk and feel sorry for yourself. Then you tee it up the next day and hope for a couple quick birdies to bury the pain.

No, the second reason people rooted against Tiger was something a lot more reflective of human nature that all of us can

121

relate to in one fashion or another: The world is *full* of *"Coulda, Woulda, Shoulda"* people.

"Coulda, Woulda, Shoulda" people are generally frustrated with their own lives, watching it pass by, maybe trapped in a boring or dead-end job. They live in the moaning netherworld of what they *could* have done, or *should* have done, or *would* have done in a different circumstance. Jaded by their own frustrations, they root for others to fail rather than succeed.

It takes courage to change, to try something new, to follow a dream. It also takes a lot more courage than a lot of people have to find out how good – or, how not-good – they are at a given pursuit if they give it total dedication and 100% maximum effort.

Never laying it all out there always leaves a safety net for *Coulda, Shoulda, Woulda* people. That very distinctive trait, alone, prevents most Drivers from ever stepping up to becoming true Thrivers.

Thrivers relish that challenge and never back down from it. They are willing to do something to the supreme limits their skills will permit. Thrivers don't worry about losing as much as they want to win.

Most people would rather insulate themselves from feelings of failure than confront the possibility head-on. There is a beauty, a soul-cleansing purity, in knowing – for better or worse – that you tried your very best at something, regardless of whether you succeeded in the eyes and judgment of others. Your vote, the one you cast with your gut – and not their vote – is the vote that really matters.

To a Thriver, the end result isn't always the ultimate measurement. It's the journey – the courage-filled journey – which usually matters more. Courageous journeys bring courageous results and Thrivers know it.

That steely, uncompromising determination is the ultimate power of Tiger Woods. Tiger has no real use for *Coulda, Woulda, Shoulda* people. Like virtually all Thrivers, Tiger subscribes to the

No Stinkin' Thinkin' school of positive thought. If ever there was a tall wiry poster-child to the power of confidence, vision, and preparation, it's young Mr. Woods.

Tiger's legions of fans continue to grow, tournament after tournament, not just because of what he does but how he goes about doing it. He is never satisfied with being better yesterday than he was today.

A great example grew out of Tiger's win at Augusta in the 1997 Masters when he won his first major championship – the most coveted title in golf.

He decided his swing, the same swing that lofted him to a record-setting 12-shot victory margin, wasn't good enough. His vision, his goal, was to eclipse the records of the great Jack Nicklaus.

In order to do that, Tiger believed he needed to get better. Tiger did not think the status quo was performance-proofed enough for the long haul. He was determined to follow his passion for continuous improvement. Despite his startling and unprecedented win at the Masters, Tiger believed he needed to get better.

Woods decided he needed to develop a new swing, and with it a different game. He wanted a different swing that was fundamentally simple and sound, robotically dependable, and replicatable for the long haul. He needed to remove wildness from his game and pressure-proof his ball-striking.

So, he did what nobody in his or her right mind would do. Tiger Woods, Masters Champion, dismantled his record-setting swing and set out to build a different one.

Golf's history books are littered with horror stories of past champions who tried to do the same thing and failed. And a golf swing is much like a scorned lover. Once they're gone, they rarely come back as loving as before.

For Woods, rebuilding his entire swing might not have been going all the back to Square One, but it was Square Two or Three.

123

It was almost like a young salmon spotting all the adults a halfway up-the-river lead and then deciding to beat them back up to the spawning grounds just to try and do it.

Tiger basically dismantled all key parts of his swing, from grip to balance to how far he took the club back – just about everything – and then, with coach Butch Harmon helping him, decided exactly *how* the desired state for each component *should* be.

Tiger went through several months of frustration, and maybe some periodic gum-scrapes of self-doubt, but never strayed from the single-minded and dogged determination of reaching his goal. Then, one day on the range, *IT* happened. He felt it in his hands, brain, toes and soul, all simultaneously. *IT* clicked. He'd built the swing he set out to build.

Thus energized, Woods pounded balls until a lesser man – or woman – would've screwed themselves waist-deep in the driving range sod.

Tiger was doing what every smart Thriver does: He was building equity in himself – ball-striking confidence with the new swing – so that when showtime came, he would never be in a spot to hit a shot he hadn't already hit perfectly a thousand times before with his confident, new, tournament-ready golf swing. Tiger used hard work and preparation to pressure-proof his game.

The results – the validation of his determined recommitment to maximizing his potential – have been extraordinary to say the least.

The Tiger Woods popularity pendulum now, of course, has begun its ever-widening swing to the good side – where it belongs. The pro-Tiger camp swells with each sensational victory as more and more of the *Coulda, Shoulda, Woulda* people realize what they should've known all along – that life's better if we all root for each other to succeed, rather than fail. Rooting for others to fail is a selfish pettiness with no positive purpose.

People now *want* to see Tiger take it to the limit. To see if he can, in fact, break the records of the great Nicklaus, all the while laughing and teasing the little kids who adore him, and all-the-while maintaining his ever-ascending role as the global ambassador of a sport whose growth he is single-handedly magic-wanding.

There is no *"Can't Because"* in Tiger Woods. He's the most positive thinking guy on the planet. He's a *"How Can We?"* guy, not a *"Can't Because"* guy. Tiger sees only success – truly a great lesson for us all, learned from the young Jedi knight who uses laser-accurate irons instead of a light saber.

What makes Tiger Woods so great at what he does are his savvy and disciplined persistence to be the very best Tiger Woods can be at what he's chosen to do. He pursues knowledge like a doctoral student, sharpens his skills with the urgency of a gladiator, and stays true to the Daily Dozen he's created that nurture his attributes.

Tiger, like Martha Stewart, is a penultimate Thriver. He is a remarkably singular talent, certainly, but each of us is quite capable of "Tigerizing" certain segments of our life that matter greatly to us.

While there's only one Tiger Woods and one Martha Stewart, Thrivers dot the all-star performance rosters of nearly every organization.

Thrivers, by nature, act. They leave footprints rather than buttprints on the beaches of time. When Ted Turner spoke at Notre Dame's commencement address and told the crowd rather bluntly, "You don't have to know anything to make something happen," Turner's message was that the most important thing for those young adults to do was make footprints – make things happen – regardless of whether or not those prints walked across the sand in a straight line.

Thrivers adapt and change over time. They have to. In order to achieve all the goals they hope to achieve, Thrivers live with a sense of grateful urgency as the seasons of their lives mature.

Thrivers are well aware they have a finite amount of time to get done what they want in life – both personally and professionally. Consequently, most Thrivers are very good time managers.

Thrivers can be concept or detail-oriented. They may or may not know the average U.S. male lives 72.3 years and the average U.S. female lives 79.1 years, but they *do know* that time is an irreplaceable, finite, ever-diminishing resource.

They realize that years are comprised of days and each sundown marks another grain of sand dropped from the top to the bottom of their life's hourglass.

Thrivers keep one eye on their goals in life and the other on that hourglass. Thrivers are quite aware that all the money in the zip code can't buy back even one single grain of gravity-dropped sand. Consequently, Thrivers zealously protect their time preciously, like a lost camper shielding a last-match flame on a cold and windy night.

Thrivers realize that bad habits leak sand and waste a lot of granules. Ongoingly, Thrivers consciously try and shore up any leakage. They also are ever-vigilant against time robbers – activities with a poor payoff for the amount of time invested.

Time robbers can wear shoes, too. Thrivers know to politely push-back, quickly, when interrupted. If it's an emergency, they handle it; if it's important, they schedule it; if it's neither, they say no and won't waste time on it.

And Thrivers don't shortchange themselves. They figure out the number one thing they want headlined in their obituary and then bust their butts to live a life that helps write that headline in big black capital letters.

But for everything a Thriver is, there's also something important she or he isn't.

A Thriver *isn't* a special, magical or pre-ordained individual. They are regular people who've honed their skills to shed distractions and learned how to get more desired results than

126

others. They made and honor an ongoing personal commitment to maximize their own unique set of talents.

Thrivers are made, not born. *If you want to be one, you can become one.* Thrivers continually strive to increase their Knowledge, hone their Skills, and demonstrate leadership Attributes.

Soon we'll examine individually each of those vital three ingredients – Knowledge, Skills and Attributes ("KSA's") – and the role they play in living a high-performance lifestyle. But first, we'll examine the other two types of performers: The Surviors and Drivers.

"Survivors"

A quick glance at the *Thriver, Survivor & Driver* description chart earlier in the chapter succinctly sums up the dubious traits of a Survivor. Few Thrivers hang out with Survivors. They live in two different and separate orbits and rarely have too much – except perhaps a hobby – in common.

But being a Survivor isn't necessarily a life sentence. To a person motivated to improve their life, being at the bottom rung of a ladder is nothing more than a starting point from which to shove off and start the persistent climb of personal achievement.

There are some tremendous stories surrounding superstars who overcame tough obstacles to lift themselves up and out of a Survivor environment.

One of the greatest examples in modern American history is Oprah Winfrey. If ever *anyone* was born with an excuse to live a life in Survivor anonymity, it was Oprah.

But someone forgot to tell her, and Oprah's positive impact on the lives of others is absolutely remarkable – fairy tale stuff that continues to exponentially blossom in new and tremendously positive ways.

Oprah Winfrey's an African-American woman born out of wedlock who had a premature child of her own, also out of wedlock, by the age of 14.

The infant died.

Oprah was a good student, but a "wild-child" at home. The only thing that kept her out of a juvenile hall was the lack of an available bed.

After the loss of her baby, Oprah's father and stepmother moved to Nashville. She took full advantage of a second chance, starting over and beginning what would be an upward one-way elevator ride from being a Survivor, to Driver, to penultimate Thriver.

The winner of the Millennium 2000 Spingarn Medal, awarded by the NAACP for the highest achievement by a black American the previous year, Oprah's selection followed such fellow American icons as George Washington Carver (1923), Marian Anderson (1939), Martin Luther King, Jr. (1964), and Colin Powell (1991).

Her self-propelled journey from seeming despair and the cellar of poverty to becoming one of the richest and most influential women in American history underscores the startling power of what a talented and determined person can do once she (or he) puts their hard-working mind to it.

Three years after the troubled young teenager moved to Nashville, Oprah earned a college scholarship. Two years later, at 19, Oprah became the first African-American to anchor the news on Nashville's WTVF-TV. She stayed there three years, then moved to Baltimore to host the 6-o'clock evening news.

A year later, Oprah got busted down – she was taken out of the anchor spot and demoted to morning talk show host. Oprah stayed on the Baltimore talk show for four years, then moved in 1984 to host "A.M Chicago." The show was renamed after her the following year and went into national syndication.

Oprah's meteoric rise to stardom still hasn't peaked. Her financial wealth continues to compound to stratospheric levels. By 1996, Oprah was the first woman to top Forbes Top 40 Entertainers list, which ranked the industry by income. She was the only entertainer and lone African-American on Forbes' list of the 400 richest Americans.

Despite her staggering fame and financial success, Oprah's message and core values remain virtually unchanged. She lives each day married to her Daily Dozen.

"The message has always been the same," she said in a recent interview with Newsweek. "(and that's) That *you* are responsible for your life." Oprah then went on to discuss picking life's best path to follow.

"I don't think of myself as a good businesswoman," she said modestly. "I am a person who is aware of what my purpose is and what my gifts are.

"And what I teach is that if you are strong enough and bold enough to follow your dreams, then you will be led in the path that is best for you. The voices of the world will drown out the voice of God and your intuition if you let it."

Oprah then added a vitally important point: "And most people are directed by voices outside themselves."

Another very interesting facet of how this dynamic leader thinks is her view on the importance of long-range planning. In short, compared to many others, she doesn't do much of it. She puts a lot more trust in following her feelings. Remember: When we talk about success formulas, everyone's is different.

Instead of following a detailed strategic plan, Oprah implicitly trusts her internal instincts to pursue what makes her happy – and trusts those instincts will draw the right road map for her to follow.

Oprah has found her success formula and has supreme confidence that by executing her Daily Dozen – her defined and personally bought-into core values – she will be at peace internally. She trusts that inner peace – her passport to a busy, demanding yet contented life – to deliver good things for her and others.

She lives an active, visible and very caring life – yet very much with a Pro Leisure Tour attitude. Oprah controls what she worries about and what she doesn't, trusts her judgment on issues important to her, and strives to help improve the lives of others.

Oprah's long-time beau, Steadman Graham, is a near-fanatic about setting goals, managing his calendar, and allocating his time.

"Well," said Oprah. "I am just none of that. I live moment to moment."

A further glimpse inside this special talent came during her commencement speech a few years ago at Wellesley College. Oprah spoke of five important lessons she'd learned on the road from wayward teenager to national role model. Her key message points urged the students to have the courage to search deeply for their own identity and trust what they found.

"Become more fully who you are," she told them. "That inner voice that told me that you need to try to find a way to answer to your own truth was the voice I needed to be still and listen to."

The next point Oprah made came from her long-time mentor (whom she mentioned and thanked) – Maya Angelou. "When people show you who they are," urged Oprah, "believe them, the first time.

"Live your life from truth and you will survive everything, *everything*, I believe – even death. That took me awhile to get," she continued, "pretending to be something I wasn't, wanting to be somebody I couldn't, but understanding deep inside myself when I was willing to listen, that my own truth and *only* my own truth could set me free."

Next, Oprah talked about overcoming adversity. "Turn your wounds into wisdom," she said. "You will be wounded many times in your life. You'll make mistakes. Some people will call them failures but I have learned that failure is really God's way of saying, "*Excuse me*, you're moving in the wrong direction.

"It's just an experience," she added, "Just an experience."

Oprah then spoke about her career set-back at the Baltimore TV station. Basically, she was bounced off the news because she cried during sad stories.

The Baltimore demotion, she said, taught her all about passion. "It wasn't until I was demoted as an on-air anchorwoman and thrown into the talk show arena to get rid of me, that I allowed my own truth to come through.

"The first day I was on the air doing my first talk show back in 1978, it felt like breathing, which is what your true passion should feel like. It (passion) should be *so* natural to you."

Oprah then talked about the importance of coupling gratitude with a positive attitude – being nice and being good to others. She also mentioned her journal – a written log of her life since she was 15 years old.

She openly talked about her diary to the graduates, urging them all to begin keeping one and to write down five positive things each day they should be grateful for.

"I believe that if you can learn to focus on what you have, you will always see that the universe is abundant and you will have more. If you concentrate and focus in your life on what you don't have, you will never have enough. Be grateful."

Lastly, Oprah talked about the importance of defining what you wanted to be in life. Her message was clear: Think big and never underestimate yourself.

"Create the highest, grandest vision possible for your life because you become what you believe," she urged. "Every life speaks to the power of what can be done. Hold the highest vision possible for your life and it *can* come true."

The Oprah Winfrey who addressed the graduating class at Wellesley that day is the same knee-high Mississippi farm girl who watched her grandmother boil clothes in a big, bubbling iron pot because the family had no washer.

Oprah knew then – at the age of four or five as she watched through an old screen door – that her life could be bigger and better than what she saw. Oprah didn't know how much bigger or how much better, but she knew she it *could* be. And she decided it *would* be.

As it turns out, young Oprah was very much correct.

Being a Survivor is not a crime. Or a condemnation. It can be lily pad for the motivated to hop on to get their bearings, then hop off of en route to swimming toward a more fulfilling life that includes working hard to achieve far greater things.

Often a Survivor simply needs a reason, an impetus – a mentor, perhaps – to change their life for the better. Usually what's missing are goals, a passion to attain them, a pride to pursue them, and a self-esteem that expects success.

Goals can be created, passion can be found, pride can be developed and self-esteem can rise from the ashes of uncertainty after just a few small, encouraging successes – especially when steered by a concerned friend, loving family member, caring co-worker or helpful mentor.

If you see someone who's reaching out for help – then eagerly volunteer to reach in and help. Change a life for the better.

But not every Survivor *is* motivated to change. Some simply don't care. They don't care about themselves, their work or others around them.

If someone *doesn't* want help, then reach out and mentor someone else. Even the most determined of cowboys can't pull a stubborn mule uphill.

(Chevrolet) "Drivers"

Most folks are Drivers, which is a good thing. They constitute the big middle portion of the bell curve and serve to make the world go-round. They are the assembly line that keeps

132

repopulating our businesses and communities with ever-precious Thrivers.

Drivers are people with talent and solid core values who can develop into great leaders by using the growth opportunities that surround them. Things like:

♦ Capitalizing on pro-active learning opportunities by using resources, mentors and role models for specific and clearly-understood reasons.

♦ Making a heartfelt commitment – to themselves – that being average just isn't good enough and accepting greater responsibility and with it increased accountability.

♦ Shunning bad habits and rechanneling that valuable recaptured time, energy, and money into activities that build increased personal equity.

♦ Learning from mistakes and avoiding preventable encores.

♦ Insisting that some sort of passion maintains a highly-visible role and threads throughout daily life.

♦ Focusing on the truly important – which means worrying *only* about things Drivers truly should – and volunteering to try things that at first blush appear quite difficult but are worthwhile pursuing.

The quality list could go on and on but Drivers *are* impressionable. That's *good news* when Drivers are surrounded by Thrivers and immersed in positive, motivating environments. Thrivers can hoist a Driver up into a higher level of performance.

Being impressionable is *bad news* if Drivers are surrounded by Survivors and immersed in negative, selfish or manipulating environments. Survivors can pull a Driver right back down, especially attitudinally.

If we know what we are – and what we truly and deep-down aspire to be – then life's given us a green light to chase our dreams. How fast we choose to drive toward becoming a Thriver is, well, pretty much our own individual decision.

So, put the car in gear and get going. The engine that powers the drive from *Survivor* to *Driver* to *Thriver* contains three primary components:

1. *"Knowledge,"*
2. *"Skills,"* and
3. *"Attributes"*

These three things – *Knowledge, Skills* and *Attributes* ("KSA's") – are dissected in detail in our next chapter. Each has a very specific contributing relationship that helps determine whether someone is a Thriver, Survivor or Driver.

Sustained success is never an accident. It's a _byproduct_. And the three necessary pieces of success – the KSA's – enable us to predict the probability of success with a very high degree of accuracy.

Once we understand those intertwined relationships – how Knowledge, Skills and personal Attributes mix together – we can quickly increase our effectiveness.

As a bonus, we'll also have stepped more than halfway across the river on our journey toward a more contented and effective life on the Pro Leisure Tour.

Chapter 8

KSA's & Success Probability

*"Winners are people of ordinary talent
who develop those talents to an above-ordinary degree."*
-- Theodore Roosevelt

The sheer power of this chapter is that it helps *change the way you think* about performance shortfalls at home or in the office. This is an important new thought process that comes in quite handy, quite often, on the PLT.

When you learn to think differently (and that new way of thinking becomes your automatic default logic) you will have mastered a lifelong skill that enables you to move mountains of personal achievement.

By the end of this chapter, you'll know *why* some people succeed and some don't. You will also be positioned to learn how to instantly recognize and fix whatever temporarily detours your own personal highway to success. You'll be able to quickly road map strategic plans and solutions whenever the need arises.

All these methods are important and interconnected pieces on the Pro Leisure Tour jigsaw puzzle – a puzzle already half-complete.

Our goal on the PLT is to end up with a complete mosaic of inner peace – confident in our ability to achieve worthwhile goals, troubleshoot performance issues for ourselves and others, and maintain a steady confidence that we *can* control what we do in life, how well we do it, and voluntarily help others do the same.

This chapter involves a little bit of thought-reengineering – which sounds far scarier than it is. Changing *how you think* isn't hard – it simply requires learning a new approach to analyze situations when things don't go according to plan.

135

Living Life on the Pro Leisure Tour is a blend of attitude and learned skills, and this chapter is skill-related. It focuses on changing *how* you think about performance. It helps you understand – clearly and easily – why some people succeed and others don't.

This new approach will help quickly identify, then fix, whatever might be derailing your progress en route to important achievements in personal or professional pursuits.

Best of all, by the end of this chapter, your overall effectiveness at whatever you choose to do in life should be poised to *dramatically accelerate*.

The chapter has two principle components: Understanding KSA's and Predicting Success.

Understanding KSA's

The meaty portion of the chapter deals with under-standing the key roles your *Knowledge, Skills* and *Attributes* (KSA's) play whenever you set out to achieve a specific personal or business goal.

♦ Your *Knowledge* is your relevant base of accumulated learning.

♦ Your *Skills* are your proficiency and talent level.

♦ Your *Attributes* wrap-around your intangibles – those intrinsic things that enable you to mix your Knowledge and Skills to consistently achieve desired results.

Predicting Success

Once we understand *how* KSA's blend together to create success (or cause failure), the second part of the chapter quickly and easily shows how to pretty accurately predict the probability of success.

If success proves elusive, there are three probable causes why. Each is quickly recognizable and easy to identify a fix for.

Following the investigation of the roles KSA's play in success, we'll then examine how to quickly pave over any potholes that might pop up on the road to where we want to go.

After college and the newspaper business, I spent 20 years working for Xerox. Like all big companies, every few years Xerox would have to go through a reorganization. Small ones were routine and normal. Big ones were earthquakes of disruption sprinkled with situational flakes of paranoia.

During the last half of my career, I watched the company execute two big re-orgs. One they did right.

And one they did wrong. *Really* wrong.

The one the company did right introduced us to the concept of what the company referred to as "KSA's." KSA was just one of a trillion Xerox acronyms that flew through the air like mosquitoes at a sundown barbecue. But KSA was a new acronym, and a good one.

KSA stood for Knowledge, Skills and Attributes. Everyone in the sales organization was rated on those three criteria several months in advance of the impending reorganization.

Simultaneously, each anticipated job responsibility in the new business model was mapped to a very specific and well-defined set of required talents.

In theory, by matching the necessary skill sets for the jobs with the individuals whom best demonstrated those particular skills, all jobs in the new organization would be filled with the best possible talent to produce business results at the highest possible level.

The overall success of the mapping strategy – and the minimizing of bad personnel decisions – hinged on the company's ability to do three things:

1. *Understand and define the precise requirements of each job;*

2. *Accurately (albeit subjectively) assess the Knowledge, Skills and Attributes of each worker in the affected organizations. And,*

3. *Match the two (the needs of the jobs and the skills of the people) together.*

The process wasn't perfect, but it was pretty darn good. It worked. The transition went very well, with minimal grumbling and little disruption in the field. Business continued smoothly. The company safely repositioned itself for a strategic redirection without harming either its internal or external customer base.

In fact, it's safe to say the company emerged from the far end of the tunnel in far better shape than when it entered and the repositioned key business units continued to grow profitably.

Unfortunately, the next major re-org the company tried *didn't* go so well. At the time, I likened it to the dramatic lighting of an exploding trick cigar.

This second reshuffling came about eight years after the KSA re-org. Faced with a massive, necessary restructuring and sales force realignment, the company totally abandoned the KSA-mapping approach. What resulted was political wrist-wrestling, mass confusion, and virtually zero buy-in from the troops on what was taking place.

Knowledge, Skills and Attributes were no longer valued in what proved to be a poorly-executed musical chair approach to change. Change proved a costly and ineffective mess, to say the least: Top talent defected, business results sagged dangerously, and the company's stock value plummeted like a cartoon safe freefalling out of a 10th story window toward the sidewalk below.

One of the great names in American industry caught itself in its own mousetrap.

A change in leadership at the top has enabled Xerox to re-right the internal ship and begin again moving forward. Hopefully the company will once again regain its former greatness.

Each of us has our very own set of KSA's for everything we do. We have one set for work and another set relative to each of our hobbies and interests.

First, let's better define these three important assessment traits, then synopsize each briefly:

Knowledge: *"The act, fact, or state of knowing. All that has been perceived or grasped by the mind; learning; en-lightenment."*

Knowledge, then, is the strength, width and depth of your expertise. It's your accumulated information bank – what you know that's germane to the nature of what you're trying to achieve.

Skills: *"Great proficiency. Expertness that comes from training, practice, etc. Understanding, or judgment to matter, avail, or make a difference."*

Skills refer to your specific talent level. Your best friend might know more about basketball than anyone in the world but be unable to dribble the ball without giving themselves a bloody nose. Skills, for the most part, are not natural or innate. People aren't born with skills – they are learned, developed, honed, and strengthened over time. Some skills can erode. All people have differing skill levels.

Attributes: *"A quality intrinsic, inherent, or naturally belonging to a thing or person."*

In business, demonstrated performance attributes are the rarest of the three. These are the intangibles – including subjective things like intuition, risk-taking and handling deadlines and pressure.

Attributes gauge potential and weigh the intangibles but also measure absolute performance. The applied integration of knowledge (knowing something) with skills (the talent to do something) is demonstrated by the ability of people to deliver the desired results over a sustained period of time.

Some people simply create success better and more often than others.

Can _you_ produce to a continually high level of performance? The Attributes judgment assesses motivation, proven results, and how well you continually apply the knowledge you have with the skills you possess in order to consistently achieve or (preferably) overachieve specific goals.

Great managers have the ability to astutely judge the Attributes of their people. And great performers have that same acute judgmental ability when assessing their own strengths and limitations. They know what they do better than most and are proud to continually prove it. Ego often galvanizes the unique blend of Attributes that top performers own.

Here, then, is a vitally important principle: ***In order to succeed at a particular challenge, you must have the Knowledge, Skills, and Attributes to do so.***

This awareness will come in very handy when we begin building our personal or professional strategic plans. *Thrivers* quickly and confidently mix these three success ingredients – their KSA's – like famed TV chef Emeril Lagasse effortlessly blends together a sumptuous meal. When everything is done right, the result is something special.

Quick Tips
for
Strengthening Your KSA's

Knowledge:

♦ *Accumulate learning.*
You can accelerate your progression up any expertise escalator by combining a hunger for information with an increased sense of urgency to learn. Knowledge is power – respect it accordingly. Strive to become a subject matter expert.

♦ *Read voraciously.*
Grow horizontally. The more you read the smarter you get. Broaden you knowledge base. A wide root base absorbs more water and mineral-rich nutrients to grow bigger, stronger trees.

♦ *Watch for best practices.*

By seeking a role model, you can milk the knowledge you need to glean without having to first raise the calf. Milk the knowledge, mimic the skills. Always scout for new talent to learn from. Borrow from the best.

◆ *Think.*

Think strategically and stay consciously proactive rather than reactive. I remain perpetually puzzled at the dearth of practical thought throughout way too much of corporate America. Our new sound-bite society seems to have put creative thought in a hammerlock submission hold. With so many surrounding behaviors now being interruptive and knee-jerk reactive, it's _critical_ for strategic thought to be as *proactive* as possible – and not *reactive.*

Smart, strategic analytical thinking on the front-end of a problem will always lead to the best long-term solution. Thrivers realize their competitive edge will always remain knowing one more thing than their competitors, and that it's vitally important to continually leverage that advantage in a smart, strategic and advantageous position.

If you respect the need for subject knowledge like a growing pet octopus, always remember that all arms must grow. The longer the arms, the bigger, stronger and better your octopus gets – and the better it eats. It's self-feeding – just like creative thought.

◆ *Don't be timid.*

Try and fail, if necessary. But dive in, and trust experience to be a great teacher. Hands-on effort is always a great way to learn. "Attempting" not only enhances skill development, but it serves to teach first-hand what still might need to be learned.

The first time I ever stepped in a river alone and tried to flyfish I nearly mummified myself. But I learned a lot that day that I never would've realized in a classroom – about the wind, casting rhythm, arm angles and the differences in current within a river.

I also learned a lot more about knot-tying than I planned on, too.

My charter that day wasn't proving my ineptness. I ignored that – being a streamside bungler was assumed. *My charter was to learn what else I needed to know.* And the quickest way to get an idea was to get out there and feel the experience.

Skills

♦ ***Observe the best.***

Watch what they do, ask why it's done that way, then embrace proven techniques accordingly.

Famed actress Geena Davis went to an archery competition to watch the friend of a friend compete in a national tournament. Intrigued, afterward she decided to give it a try. In just a couple years Geena became good enough to qualify for the Olympic Trials. For Geena, her passion for archery and resultant skills both started by watching the best – in action and under pressure.

♦ ***Do. Try. Succeed. Fail.***

Great talents leave little to chance. They work hard and practice with inordinate discipline.

When baseball Hall of Fame pitcher Nolan Ryan pitched his 7th no-hitter, he didn't celebrate with champagne. Nolan celebrated by riding his exercise bike in the locker room for nearly an hour. Nolan knew much of his pitching power and stamina came from his powerful legs. He also knew his skills – his competitive advantage – depended on having enough personal discipline to keep himself physically prepared at all times.

♦ ***Never be satisfied with the status quo.***

Park your ego if necessary and learn tricks and shortcuts that increase your effectiveness. Pro golfer Tiger Woods is a classic example of this point. Tiger is driven to win and determined to leave nothing in the tank while trying to do so.

Tiger has rows of empty shelves built into the wall of his home that he expects to fill with future championship trophies. He doesn't win a tournament and look for a place to put the hardware. He builds the place for the hardware and then goes out and wins it.

Innovate. Create. Avoid predictability. Practice and rehearse. Never be satisfied with the view from a rung in the middle of the ladder. Climb to the top. And if you're on the top – go get a bigger ladder. Always climb. Always change the view.

♦ *Nurture Your Creativity!*

Keep doing what you're doing and you'll keep getting what you're getting. Every step forward – every invention – comes from a better or alternative way of doing something. Nurture, challenge and use your creativity.

Creativity is latent talent for far too many. *Challenge yourself to find new and better ways of getting things done.* Be an inventor – an idea inventor. Bulldoggedly challenge yourself to invent ideas every day of your life.

Attributes

♦ *Seek high-performance role models.*

Success breeds success because successful people self-generate motivation. The more positive role models you embrace, the more you'll succeed.

All avenues of your life intersect in two places – your heart and your brain. Seek role models with inordinately magnetic personality traits. You're never too old to seek role models and never too young to be one.

♦ *Decide that winning, and achieving, really does matter.*

The ability to blend what you know with how you use your special talents in order to create desired results is judged by others based on whether you succeed or fail. Effort is always a great investment. It pays off.

To cancer-surviving bicyclist Lance Armstrong, *winning* the Tour de France meant more than simply riding in it. Winning mattered. Once he climbed the mountainous health challenge his cancer put in front of him and earned his way into the race, Armstrong tackled an even higher mountain – the challenge of winning.

143

Muhammad Ali's legacy as heavyweight champion was written by his steadfast refusal to lose to two seemingly invincible and unbeatable men: Sonny Liston and George Foreman. Ali beat both using totally different strategies. Ali had skill. And Ali has smarts. But above all, Ali had heart. Winning mattered.

◆ *Never get beat the same way twice.*
If you fail at something, learn why and commit to never being beaten the same way twice. Charles Schwab has what he calls his "Hall of Noble Failure." One of Schwab's key corporate strategies is continual innovation. Some of the brainstormed ideas are bombs bigger than *Ishtar*. Schwab cares little about the failures. The effort to innovate is what he prizes above all.

Schwab is out of the Ted Turner school of making change happen rather than *waiting* for it to happen. Like all great leaders, Charles Schwab has vision, challenges his people to find a better way, and continually makes things happen. Things might go wrong, but he doesn't make the same mistake twice. Schwab nurtures and banks on the attributes of the talent he attracts. His payoff has been a splendidly built, innovative financial management empire.

◆ *Demonstrate pride, integrity and high-road dignity in whatever you do.*
Dignity and integrity discipline people to do things right the very first time. The more done properly the first time, the less that has to be done a second time. Consequently, the discipline to do things right the first time can't help but increase your effectiveness skills.

Quality work is habit-forming. As is shoddy work.

◆ *Leverage your talents, strengthen your weaknesses.*
Wernher von Braun – the father of the American space program – flunked 9th grade algebra and was nearly as bad in physics. Fascinated by rocket science but frustrated with his inability to understand mathematics, von Braun simply decided to out-study everyone until he soon led his class in math.

He improved because he had a bulldogged determination to do so. Above all, von Braun was driven by his passion – an urgent need to learn everything possible about rocketry. He saw future possibilities for rockets way beyond where they were in his days as a student.

By the age of 22, von Braun earned a Ph.D. in physics from the University of Berlin. After Hitler's Germany surrendered to U.S. troops at the end of World War II, von Braun left Germany, came to America, and spearheaded *our* space exploration program.

He ran NASA's facility in Huntsville and became considered by many the father of NASA and the American space program. His team developed and built the massive Saturn rockets, which made modern space travel possible.

Pretty impressive stuff for a guy who refused to accept bad grades as a 9th grader.

The great thing about self-analysis of these critical assessment areas – Knowledge, Skills and Attributes – is that each lends itself to what should be unemotional objective evaluation: Either you *have* enough Knowledge or you don't. Either you *have* the required Skills or you don't. Either you've *demonstrated* the Attributes and ability to perform or you haven't.

Measured this way, success is cut, dried, simple and straightforward. The reasons for success – or failure – become brutally honest in a very great way.

All three KSA's are important. You can be *good* at something if you excel at one. And you can be *very good* at something if you're strong in two of the three.

But you've got to have all three – keen Knowledge, sharpened Skills and a winner's Attributes – in order to be *great.*

By rating someone's differing proficiencies within their KSA's, it's possible to accurately predict how successful someone's likely to be in their given pursuits.

Greatness *can* be created. Accurately assessing relevant and necessary KSA's certainly helps.

Next we'll take a look at predicting success, based on the Knowledge, Skills and Attributes of the people involved. By rating the KSA's of ourselves, employees, co-workers, or loved ones, we can – at a glance – predict how likely they are to be either a Thriver, Driver, or Survivor.

As you look at the chart, think carefully and decide where *you* fit when measured either in the office or in another setting that's important to you.

Where *do* you fit? Where you want to be or close to it?

Where would another person you know fit? How about others in the office?

Take a good look and give it some candid thought. A little self-inflicted personal dissection is always a spoon-fed vitamin for the long-term good of the soul.

Success Probability
Based on "Knowledge, Skills & Attributes"

The probability of success is fairly predictable based on different proficiency combinations of *Knowledge, Skills & Attributes*.

Knowledge and Skills are generally the easiest of the three to measure and rate. But the performance power rests in the Attributes.

Every individual has different levels of "want to." And every individual had differing combinations of intangibles. Desire helps fuel the power to perform. But desire isn't everything.

Each of us has a differing *"Potential"* for Success. And our *potential* for success is often different than the levels we actually reach. The reason why is shown below.

Potential for Success:

"Knowledge" + "Skills" = *"POTENTIAL"*

A lot of people have the knowledge and skills to succeed at things, but don't.

Knowledge plus *Skills*, combined, help measure the ***potential*** of an individual. But the world has a lot more people *with* potential than it does people reaching it.

Success Probability hinges on a person's ability to parlay their *potential* into a demonstrated ability to succeed.

Level of Success:

"Potential" x "Attributes" = *"SUCCESS LEVEL"*

A person's success will largely be a function of how they apply their special set of Attributes to their earned potential. *These Attributes are the key to sustained performance over time.*

Success Levels: *Why They Vary from Person to Person*

Knowledge and Skills *cannot measure* the "want-to," the desire, or the individual level of motivation a person needs in order to succeed. All successful people have a certain level of stubborn *"stick-to-it-iveness"* they demonstrate over extended periods of time.

People also react differently to change, pressure, setbacks and surprises.

The Attributes assessment subjectively measures those intangibles and that very subjectivity makes *Attributes* tougher to gauge than *Knowledge* (which you can do via a test) or *Skills* (often testable as well). Measuring intangibles is a lot more guess-work and intuition than science.

Attributes are *demonstrated proof* that a person's applied blend of talent and skill enables them to repeatedly complete the challenge more frequently than others.

Those special Attributes – the performance-driving things that separate Thrivers from equally knowledgeable and skilled Drivers – are the personal traits that propel people from one level of performance to the next.

Climbing a mountain is hard. But remember that it's easier to follow someone up Everest than it is to lead the expedition. Leaders – *Thrivers* – continually demonstrate that leadership ability challenge after difficult challenge.

If your life depended on following someone else's lead up Everest, my guess is you'd be a lot more comfortable doing so if that person had already repeatedly demonstrated the knowledge, skills, and leadership attributes of making those critical and necessary life-saving decisions over and over and over again.

Those proven Attributes, in a nutshell, form the difference between being able to simply *climb* Everest versus being able to lead the expedition. Thrivers lead the expedition. Drivers follow. Survivors are home on the sofa.

The following chart predicts the probability of someone being successful when three different levels of talent (low, medium and high) are mixed in varying KSA combinations. There are 27 potential skill-set combinations. You'll note:

- *Only three (3) of the 27 combinations (just 11%) create high-performing **Thrivers**.*

- *Nine (9) of the 27 (33%) produce relatively low-performing **Survivors**.*

- *The clear majority of combinations, 15 of 27 (56%), create **Drivers**.*

- *"**Attributes**" are the heaviest-weighted skills.* The reason is simple. You can teach Knowledge. And you can teach, practice, and coach Skills. Both of those categories you can directly address and improve. The hardest to drive up the effectiveness curve are the intangible-laden Attributes.

Shrewdly assessing the attributes of the people beneath you triggers the power that improves performance for any team, division, organization or corporation.

(see Success Predictability Chart on next page)

Success Predictability Chart

	Talent Mix	Knowledge Level	Skill Level	Attribute Level	Success Probability
1	LLL	Low	Low	Low	Low (Survivor; a disposable slug)
2	MLL	Medium	Low	Low	Low (Survivor; disposable)
3	HLL	High	Low	Low	Low (Survivor; disposable)
4	LML	Low	Medium	Low	Low (Survivor; disposable)
5	MML	Medium	Medium	Low	Low (Survivor; improvable)
6	HML	High	Medium	Low	Medium (Driver)
7	LHL	Low	High	Low	Low (Survivor; improvable)
8	MHL	Medium	High	Low	Medium (Driver)
9	HHL	High	High	Low	Medium (Driver)
10	LLM	Low	Low	Medium	Low (can grow)
11	MLM	Medium	Low	Medium	Low (should grow)
12	HLM	High	Low	Medium	Medium (Driver)
13	MMM	Medium	Medium	Medium	Medium (the perfect Driver)
14	MHM	Medium	High	Medium	Medium (Driver)
15	LMM	Low	Medium	Medium	Medium (Driver)
16	LHM	Low	High	Medium	Medium (Driver)
17	HMM	High	Medium	Medium	Medium (Driver)
18	HHM	High	High	Medium	Medium (Driver)
19	LLH	Low	Low	High*	Low (should grow)
20	LMH	Low	Medium	High*	Medium (Driver)
21	MLH	Medium	Low	High*	Medium (Driver)
22	MMH	Medium	Medium	High*	Medium (Driver)
23	HLH	High	Low	High*	Medium (can grow)
24	**HMH**	**HIGH**	**MEDIUM**	**HIGH***	**HIGH (THRIVER)**
25	LHH	Low	High	High*	Medium (Driver)
26	**MHH**	**MEDIUM**	**HIGH**	**HIGH***	**HIGH (THRIVER)**
27	**HHH**	**HIGH**	**HIGH**	**HIGH***	**HIGH (THRIVER; A FRANCHISE PLAYER)**

* High-attribute people are most likely to improve performance.

Success Predictability Summary:

♦ **Thrivers:**   *3 combinations.*   (#24, 26 and 27).

♦ **Drivers:**   *15 combinations.* (#6, 8, 9, 12-18, 20-23, 25).

♦ **Survivors:**   *9 combinations.*   (#1-5, 7, 10, 11, 19).

Business Relevance of Predicting Success

In business, the value of shrewd KSA assessments is enormous. If you want a group or organization or team to perform to a certain level, you simply *must* understand what fits together to produce peak performance. Results don't just happen – they occur (or don't occur) for very specific reasons.

As a manager, achieving maximum team success comes when you put your people in position to match the KSA's it takes to do the job with similar KSA's they possess.

Smart managers action-plan the gaps between the two. They create developmental escalators for their people to continually improve their Knowledge, Skills and hopefully strengthen their Attributes.

As an individual worker, you must consciously remain aware of how you stack up relative to three key things: The evolving and changing demands of your job; meeting or exceeding the expectations of others; and the expectations you hold for yourself.

Never forget that people around you measure you by what you *achieve* – not by what you *try* to achieve. Understanding *how* to leverage your unique set of KSA's for maximum performance is something each of us needs to constantly monitor.

Personal Relevance of Predicting Success

Understanding how different blends of KSAs impact results and help predict *Success Probability* should make it far easier for you to accomplish the things in life you really want to do – at the levels you hope to reach.

A second obvious and hugely beneficial tie-in is how easy it becomes for you to coach and counsel others (family, friend, relatives) in an effective, helpful, and mentoring way. KSA analysis strips away a lot of emotion from coaching and counseling sessions.

Dissecting what's wrong has a much higher chance of leading to a cure than simply guessing.

If you currently come up a bit short of the effectiveness levels you'd like to reach, now you know what to do to directly increase that effectiveness:

1. *Shore up your Knowledge by utilizing all possible resources (including human) to learn.*

2. *Strengthen your Skills by practicing, seeking and emulating role models; and proactively locating good coaches and mentors.*

3. *Embrace the reality that stronger Attributes kindle to a start from a fire within. People who <u>expect</u> themselves to succeed – will find a way to do so!*

Awareness of these things is half the challenge. Once you've got that awareness and assess your current state, figuring out what to do next is suddenly one heck of a lot easier.

By knowing what you want or need to develop – which KSA to strengthen – you have drawn a firm straight line between where you are and where you want to go. Gap closure between the two is greatly simplified.

When you've finally reached those highest levels of Knowledge, Skills and Attributes, you'll Thrive at your highest performance level. You, too, will have earned the right to lead an expedition up to the mountaintop.

Once you're the leader up the mountain rather than one of the followers, not only is the climb more fun, but your view going *up* that never-ending steep peak suddenly becomes a heck of a lot better, too.

Now that we understand the role KSA's play in the probable success of our day-to-day activities, the next chapter will take a glance at avoiding the three common things that often tackle people around the ankles as they try to move forward while trying to become Thriving top performers.

We'll scrutinize all three *"Roadblocks to Performance"* and learn how to quickly get right back on track toward where we want to be.

Once we've learned the importance of KSA's and how they relate to success, our ability to circumvent any controllable problems that pop up moves us into a position where we can analyze and pro-actively strengthen whatever might impede our progress.

Our goal is happy hopping the rest of the way across the creek and arriving safely on the shores of the PLT.

The next few chapters will lead us the rest of the way.

Chapter 9

"Uh-ohhh ...."

Roadblocks to Performance:
What to do when Things Go Wrong

When you aren't getting the results you need, one of three things went wrong. All are very common, easily identifiable and quick to develop fixes for. Best of all, the skill in ferreting out the root cause of the problem is totally *controllable* – as are the fixes.

When it comes to trying but failing, I subscribe to the theory that once is an accident, twice is a coincidence, but three or more is a trend. Understanding *why* things go wrong is a great self-improvement and mentoring tool. And being able to perform a true self-assessment is the most noble two-edged sword you'll ever impale yourself upon.

Recognizing something's gone haywire is one thing; quickly figuring out the cause is even more important. The third part of the equation is how to problem-solve a quick solution. And that's what this chapter is all about. We want to maximize efficiency.

If you aren't doing as well as you'd like, you must be able to sit down and analyze why not. The problem is being caused by one of these three things. Either you:

a) *Can't* do it.
b) *Won't* do it.
c) Or, are *Prevented From* doing it.

The first set of questions we ask ourselves when something goes wrong are always the same: "What's my problem here? Which is it? Is this simply something that I *can't* do?

"Is it something I *can* do but simply don't want to – and refuse to?

"Or is this problem something I'm capable of and willing to do, but am being *prevented from* doing it by something outside my direct control?"

Let's take a quicker and closer examination of each. At the end of this chapter are easy-to-follow flow charts that help analyze each of these three problem areas and steer you toward the right remedy quickly and easily.

Follow the flow charts until the thought process becomes automatic. Once you've analyzed a dozen or two performance shortfalls this way, the analysis process will become automatic for you. You'll instantly zip through the analytical problem-solving stage and dramatically increase your effectiveness in quickly understanding what went wrong and how to fix it.

Is the Problem a "*Can't* Do It?"

A *Can't Do It* becomes evident when someone simply does not demonstrate the ability to successfully complete the challenge at hand. A *"can't do it"* is either a knowledge or skill problem – it's one or the other. Assuming you're doing something within your means, a *can't do it* is usually fixable. Knowledge can be learned; training can enhance skills; and frequent practice can usually help deliver the desired level of expertise and performance.

Unfortunately, sometimes all the knowledge and training in the world will not permit someone without the correct skill set to do a job properly. I can't dunk a basketball. I know how, but gravity significantly outweighs my desire.

"Can't do it" problems are either caused by Knowledge deficiencies (controllable and fixable) or Skill deficiencies (sometimes fixable, sometimes not). You have to figure out which it is, then devise the appropriate remedy. My inability to dunk is a skill deficiency. The remedy is a mini-tramp or lower rim.

Legal career counselor Murphy Reed from Austin, Texas is quick to point out that in his two decades of management experience, people eager to succeed often don't even realize *what* they need to know in order to succeed. It sounds trite but, in Reed's view, sometimes people simply don't know…..what they don't know.

"Sometimes people need help determining *what* knowledge is required for success," he said. In those cases, Reed steers his people toward all available resources – including Thrivers, who typically are proud to mentor someone eager to succeed.

"Every challenge in life has a success formula," said Reed. "Accumulated knowledge can come from a thousand sources, and successful people seek it out, then test their understanding with people who've already traveled the road they're on.

"The ones who don't succeed," he added, "are those who never utilize resources – human or otherwise. Without testing and *validating* your own understanding of what you need to know, then all you're ever doing is hoping and trying."

Or is the Problem a *"Won't* Do It?"

Anyone with the ability to achieve something but for whatever reason chooses *not to* falls into this category. Generally, there are only two reasons someone *won't* do something they are capable of doing:

1. Human nature steers people to avoid things they don't like doing. If the requested task is unpleasant and there's no punishment associated with failing to doing it, there's no real reason for a person to have to comply. *Or,*

2. There's no suitable reward or incentive for doing it. Nothing is gained, so why bother? Just because someone is capable of doing something doesn't mean they'll automatically want to. Most folks, especially at work, need an incentive. Incentives can be positive *or* negative.

As a parent or manager, simply installing suitable penalties or rewards typically eliminates a *"Won't do it"* as a performance barrier. If neither solves the problem, a private discussion will usually ferret out the real reason for non-performance very quickly.

Both punishments and rewards should match the size of the challenge. Consider both a short-term tactical fix. We need to create an environment where these issues are eliminated, not perpetuated.

Of the three categories *(Can't, Won't, or Prevented From)*, the *"Won't Do Its"* are usually the easiest of the three barriers to quickly recognize and fix.

Be cautious about a malady called "performance punishment." Sometimes people don't want to do something because they're good at it – and since they're good at it, they have to do it more often than others who aren't.

For example, a former meatcutter in a grocery store is a pretty handy person to have around during Thanksgiving. And that's OK. But put the same person in a hunting camp and he might get stuck cleaning every animal every hunter brought in simply because he knew how and no one else cared to learn.

That's no fun for anyone stuck on the brandishing end of the blade and a vivid real-world example of performance punishment. Just because someone is good at something doesn't mean they should always have to do it all the time, when others are quite capable of learning.

Procrastinators are often *Won't Do It* people. For them, a suitable reward or punishment is often required. Parents use similar techniques every single day with the kids. Use the same philosophy – introducing punishment and reward commensurate with the expectation – as a spur in the butt to help a person move forward with something they are clearly capable of doing but choosing not to.

But the goal is always to eliminate the negative behavior, not feed it or perpetually punish a repeat offender. By eliminating the problem, performance nearly always improves.

Or is this a "**_Prevented From_**" Issue?

"*Prevented Froms*" occur when someone with the knowledge, skills and attributes to do something is unable to succeed because of uncontrollable circumstances.

For example, someone might not show up for an important 5 o'clock meeting because child care closes at 5:30. Or tickets to a sold-out show go unused because of a traffic accident that wasn't your fault.

Or, perhaps a reading tutorial might be too difficult for a loyal worker with dyslexia. The great actor, producer and director Henry Winkler is dyslexic and has had to develop workarounds his entire show business career. Dyslexia didn't stop Winkler from graduating from an Ivy League college or becoming a huge worldwide star. Thrivers like Winkler *always* figure out a way to win.

In each of these three examples, there was an uncontrollable reason that prevented someone from doing something they would normally have done.

All top performers seek workarounds to barriers, relentlessly so in positive environments.

People are far less loyal and far less likely to seek workarounds in excuse-riddled, manipulative, or negative types of environments.

So, whether you're at home with the family or working late in the office, whenever something doesn't go according to plan, stop to analyze why. The appropriate fix depends on your determination:

1. Either they person *can't do it* and need more knowledge or skill development;

2. They *won't do it* and need a suitable reward or punishment en route to creating an environment where these issues are eliminated.

159

3. Or, they are being *prevented from doing it* and need help either removing the barriers or thinking up a workaround.

How to Fix what Breaks

Here are some helpful success tips:

♦ **Have, and _execute_, a well thought-out plan.**

When you've developed a sound strategy but are running into some setbacks, *don't panic.* Stay the course. Recognize what broke, then fix it, learn from it and resume hustling. Sometimes setbacks are nothing more than a blizzard of bugs splatted on your strategic windshield. A temporary inconvenience. Pull over, clean the glass, gas up, and hop back in the car. Resume driving toward your destination.

♦ **The more time and careful strategic thought you put into developing your plan, the fewer barriers you'll bump into.**

It takes more cerebral energy to strategize where in life or business you're headed – and to draw the map – than it does to aimlessly wander around. After 30 years befriending and mentoring talented executives, retired Xerox training manager George Simmons weighed in succinctly on the topic.

"Most people spend more time planning their summer vacations than they do their careers," George said. "Don't know why, but they do. Think about it."

Any time you're traveling toward a goal worth pursuing, a carefully crafted map in-hand, negotiating potholes and detours along the way is nothing more than minor delays en route to your final destination. But driving blind – without that map – means you'll never know where the shortcuts are.

Most people drive 52 miles from Telluride, Colorado to the scenic alpine town of Ouray. The smart ones, however, drive only 18. The road's a little bumpier, but the scenery's better and so is the traffic – or joyful lack thereof.

♦ ***Know what you are and what you aren't; what you can do and what you can't.***

Try and stay between the boundaries of your capabilities. If you can accurately assess your knowledge and skill levels, you'll avoid falling into the trap of trying to be all things to all people. When you try to do *that*, generally you end up being nothing to anyone.

Worst of all, your self-esteem will take a bit of beating because your conscience will send sporadic nastygrams complaining about the boulder you're attempting to roll uphill by committing to expectations obviously beyond the effective scope of your capabilities.

Your conscience is your built-in chiding device. Don't activate it if you can avoid it. The thing beeps forever, like an alarm clock you can't figure out how to shut off.

The more you consciously strengthen your KSA's, the fewer roadblocks you'll run into:

♦ Adding *Knowledge* builds perpetual equity in yourself. Do it at every opportunity.

♦ Your *Skills* sharpen from pride and practice. Hone them to the best of your ability.

♦ *Attributes* will always be measured by your talent merging what you know with your ability to execute your plans. Raise the bar of what you expect of yourself and your attributes will strengthen commensurately.

Recap

When you hit a bump in the road, quickly step back and cut to the heart of the issue. What's the *real* reason: Is it a <u>can't</u> do; a <u>won't</u> do, or a <u>*prevented from*</u>?

If you <u>*can't*</u> do it, seek resources to teach you how. If you'll never have the necessary talent, acknowledge it. Less than 1% of college baseball players reach the major leagues. *Less than half who reach the majors* are good enough to stay for five years. Sometimes our limited physical capabilities prevent us from attaining our greatest dreams.

If the problem traces to a *won't* do it, the immediate question to ask is "Why not?"

What's lacking? The reward? The penalty? Or is it a case of performance punishment?

And lastly, if you're *prevented from* doing something, develop a practical workaround to circumvent the problem. Create an alternative solution. Everest is the world's tallest mountain and all successful climbers end up in the same place – at the summit. But there are several different routes to get there. None are easy but there's always more than one route to every successful expedition.

From time to time all of us need to help others navigate situational darkness. Above all, never panic. Stay the course and achieve what you set out to achieve!

On the following pages are three flow charts to quickly help pinpoint the probable cause of performance problems.

Take the time to think of a recent performance challenge you've faced. Look at each chart, think carefully about your own issue and decide what caused the problem.

Then follow the appropriate cause down further in search of solution remedies. Once you've followed it all the way through, repeat the exercise with a different challenge faced by a friend or co-worker.

With practice, this "decision tree" way of analyzing performance issues will become automatic – a reflexive logic you automatically engage whenever you face a problem-solving opportunity. It's a valuable talent to master and a wonderful tool to teach others, too. Learning to think this way is a valuable life skill that with just a little bit of practice will truly become automatic.

Invest the time. It'll pay you back a thousand-fold.

Barriers to Performance

"_Knowledge,_ Skills or Attributes?"

Which is it? Is the problem a _Knowledge_ issue?

Chart Objective: Analyzing whether the performance problem stems from a _Knowledge_ issue.

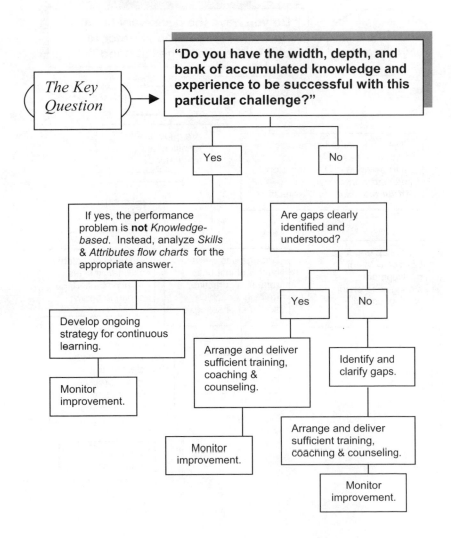

The Key Question

"Do you have the width, depth, and bank of accumulated knowledge and experience to be successful with this particular challenge?"

Yes

No

If yes, the performance problem is **not** _Knowledge-based_. Instead, analyze _Skills & Attributes flow charts_ for the appropriate answer.

Are gaps clearly identified and understood?

Yes

No

Develop ongoing strategy for continuous learning.

Monitor improvement.

Arrange and deliver sufficient training, coaching & counseling.

Identify and clarify gaps.

Monitor improvement.

Arrange and deliver sufficient training, coaching & counseling.

Monitor improvement.

Barriers to Performance:

Knowledge, *Skills* or Attributes?

Which is it? Is the problem a Skills issue?

Chart Objective: Analyzing whether the performance problem stems from a *Skill* issue.

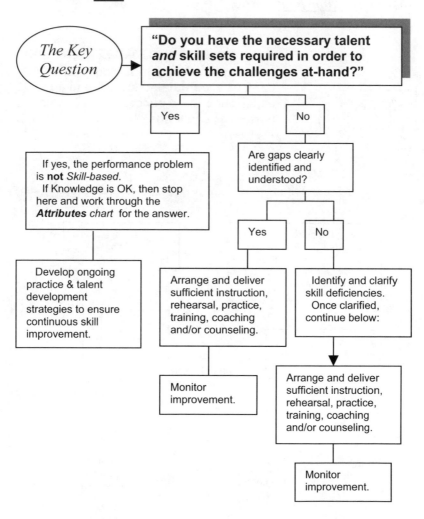

The Key Question

"Do you have the necessary talent *and* skill sets required in order to achieve the challenges at-hand?"

Yes

No

If yes, the performance problem is **not** *Skill-based*.
If Knowledge is OK, then stop here and work through the ***Attributes** chart* for the answer.

Are gaps clearly identified and understood?

Yes

No

Develop ongoing practice & talent development strategies to ensure continuous skill improvement.

Arrange and deliver sufficient instruction, rehearsal, practice, training, coaching and/or counseling.

Identify and clarify skill deficiencies. Once clarified, continue below:

Monitor improvement.

Arrange and deliver sufficient instruction, rehearsal, practice, training, coaching and/or counseling.

Monitor improvement.

Barriers to Performance:

Knowledge, Skills or *Attributes?*

Which is it? Is it an Attributes issue?

Chart Objective: To help analyze whether the performance problem stems from an *Attribute* issue.

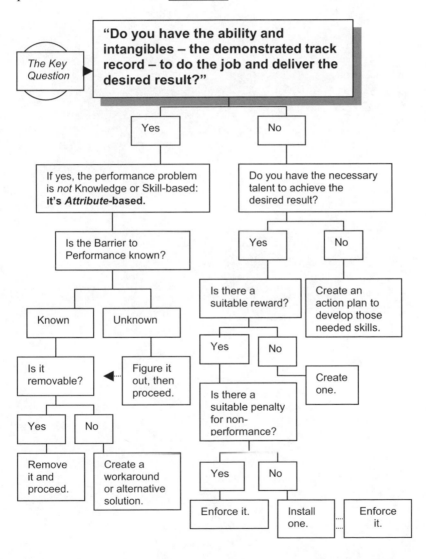

Section Three:

THE

FUTURE

The Octagon of Mediocrity

Big Ears & Lofty Dreams

Making the Impossible Possible

"LIFE" IS A 4-LETTER WORD

Closing the Studio Door

A Final Word

Chapter 10

The Octagon of Mediocrity

Self-assessment is like looking in a mirror: It's a tough thing to do objectively. But carefully measuring your Knowledge, Skills and Attributes is critically important if you want to remain clearly focused on what it takes to reach a very important goal.

To complement the correlation between KSA's and success probability, we'll now take a quick look at *The Octagon of Mediocrity*. The Octagon deals with eight common behavioral aspects that can act as walls, or barriers, to becoming a *Thriver*.

Thrivers perform at high levels because they have the Knowledge and Skills to succeed, and apply them with a set of winning Attributes. When Thrivers *don't* get the results they want, they have the smarts to step back, identify the root cause of the reason (whether the derailment stemmed from a Can't, Won't, or Prevented From issue) and stridently take the necessary action steps to fix it.

Thrivers perceive setbacks to be detours, not roadblocks. Thrivers maneuver around the detour and get back onto their clearly mapped-out road to success.

Thrivers also refuse to stay trapped behind any of the eight walls of the Octagon of Mediocrity.

Take a look at the chart on the next page and see if any of these very common barriers look familiar.

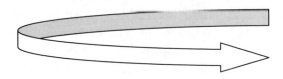

The Octagon of Mediocrity

8 Invisible Walls that Create *"Mimes of the Mediocre"*

Too many people tolerate invisible walls that keep them from achieving their true potential. For example, many folks born into a middle class environment see it as a comfort zone and are content to stay in it as they, like their parents, age through adulthood. For some reason, they don't envision themselves capable of upper echelon success.

But Thrivers aren't happy with a life of status quo. Thrivers climb ladders and they enjoy the changing view with every single step. They move up. And on. And out.

Every one of us is an individual laboratory of unique opportunity! Life does not pre-ordain boundaries. None of us are born into a caste system where we're slave to our birthrights. And, like scientists in a lab, each one of us has our own unique formula for maximum performance and another one for personal fulfillment and contentment. The closer the two formulas overlap, the fewer extra ingredients you need to fulfill both.

170

None of us can change where we're from – but we _all_ can change where we're going and how we get there.

The Eight Walls

The Octagon of Mediocrity has eight invisible walls. One by one, here are eight things you need to make certain to watch out for:

Wall #1: *You Don't Know Yourself.*

Knowing yourself requires true, deep, and sometimes soul-searching introspection. Reality can be a very cruel mirror when you remove your masks and makeup and look to the fiber of every facet of your personal and professional life. The better you know yourself, the easier it is to improve your skills and life.

Do you know which of the seven primary personality types you are? Are you an *independent* – self-motivated and capable of going off on your own and succeeding? Or are you a *compliant* – someone who's obedient and does what they're told without question? Perhaps you're an *attention-seeker* – a person who thrives on being the center of attention. *Attention-seekers* often dress and behave loudly or insist on arriving and departing according to their own clock. Some are bedecked with a ton of flashy jewelry.

Hopefully you're not a *sniper* – a low-key, negative sort that says very little but specializes in negative comments. Just as bad the opposite way is the *hero*. A hero is a know-it-all and bombastically proud to share that wonderful news with everyone – whether they care to hear it or not.

Perhaps you're just a *silent* – someone quiet by nature who's reluctant to contribute to discussions even if you can, just as reluctant to ask for help even if you need it. Hopefully you're not an *anxious dependent*. AD's worry about everything under the sun and are scared to do much of anything without permission.

171

I was lucky enough to learn about these personality types back when I taught at the Xerox Training Center. Knowing what type of individuals we were working with gave us a big edge in maximizing our effectiveness as instructors.

It helps to know your personality type. Often, it will steer you toward how you most effectively go about strengthening your KSA's.

There are correlations between personality types and success but there are no absolutes. A personality type is the method to the madness. Performance results still will always default back to how each individual responds to knowing that success will come from blending their Knowledge, Skills and Attributes into their own personal winning formula.

Truthfully knowing yourself (both pluses and minuses) means knowing whether or not you have the knowledge to succeed. Do you have the talent? The ability? How do you handle failing? Are you motivated by yourself, by others, by fear, or by success? Or are you not even sure *what* specifically motivates you?

Do you flourish or fold under pressure? Do you even care? Does winning matter? Does losing? Can you feed your ego without compromising the Daily Dozen core values that identify who you want to be? Will you bend a core value for cash?

If there are things in life you want to do but struggle to achieve, can you pinpoint which of the three probable causes it is? Is it that you *can't* do something, for whatever reason *won't* do it, or are frustratingly *prevented* from doing it? Can you root cause the specific reason why? Can you figure out the fix on your own, or should you ask for help? If you need help, will you proactively seek it out rather than wait for someone to ask if you need it?

More importantly, do you have the personal courage to fix whatever's broken? It takes a *thousand times* more courage to admit to ourselves that others are better than us at something than it does to pretend they're just lucky, not good, and choose instead to never do a thing to shore up our weaknesses.

Nearly *all* personal shortcomings are fixable. But if they weren't hard to fix, they wouldn't be broken in the first place.

Introspection is sort of like a dark basement closet. It's sometimes hard to go in there alone, especially if you haven't been inside for awhile. But there are no monsters in the closet and there aren't any inside of you either.

Self-examination, if you have the courage to dig deep enough to hit the very bedrock of your being, is a very good thing. It provides strength, character and confidence. Use your resources, lean on comrades, and reality-test with trusted others.

Wall #2:

You Run the Race on the Hamster Wheel to Nowhere.

The Hamster Wheel is the squeaky life treadmill so many of us take turns running around. I know some furious runners. But no matter how fast you run, the wheel keeps squeaking yet takes you nowhere.

Running the wheel can keep you busy but it *cannot* make you productive. Remember that activities don't necessarily produce results. Minimize the time you waste running laps on The Hamster Wheel to Nowhere. And if you unavoidably get stuck running, be cognizant of its wasteful futility and look to hop off as soon as possible.

Want to know if you're on it? An old adage leaps to mind: "Keep doing what you're doing and you'll keep getting what you're getting." If you find yourself working harder (or longer) with the same or less results – chances are, you're on it.

If your work or life is unfulfilling and a Pro Leisure Tour attitude about living is so far off in the distance you can barely see the outline of the palm trees – then chances are, you're on it.

Worst of all, if your day-to-day living isn't fueled by a passion for something that really matters to you, either personally *or* professionally – well, that squeaky wheel you're hearing is caused by your very own footsteps. Obviously, you're on it.

Look for a way to hop off. *Quickly!* Don't stay trapped on the Hamster Wheel to Nowhere!

Wall #3:

You Don't Know Why Being Average Stinks.

Being average stinks for one hugely simple reason – you're just as close to the bottom as you are to the top. I heard or read that somewhere and never, ever forgot it.

Avoid the mediocrity trap. Thrivers in life are never happy being mediocre when they have the talent to step up and play at a higher level.

Never accept being a faux leather belt in the wardrobe of the average human. Strive to be an expensive shirt or nice piece of jewelry. Strive to be valuable. Be valuable at home, in the office, and in the community.

Stay unbiased when assessing your own talents relative to others. Be *more* determined to maximize your potential than others. Be closer to the top than the bottom. Strive to be top-shelf in everything you do.

Wall #4:

You Don't Believe in Earning the Right to Succeed or Fail.

Whenever you've paid the price to succeed or fail at something new, relish the opportunity and take it. Any veteran marathon runner will tell you the same thing: Getting to the finish line isn't hard. What's *hard* is earning the right to reach the starting line.

When you've run 1,000 practice miles preparing to run 26 on race day, you have earned the right to toe the line. You have

174

earned the right to succeed or fail. Chances are you will succeed, as most marathon starters do. They succeed because they have earned the right to succeed. They've paid the price.

Every smart manager is unwavering in her or his support of people who've earned a new opportunity. The same holds true in social circles.

There's a heck of a big difference between earning an opportunity and simply being handed one. If someone believes you've earned a chance, they also believe you've got the KSA's to deliver. Prove them right.

When you attempt those things in life you've earned the right to try, chances are you will do them very well and with a great degree of confidence. The trick is to keep earning the right to do more.

Wall #5:

You'd Rather be a Role Player than an Impact Player.

Many years ago I watched a TV interview of baseball player Brady Anderson. Brady hit 51 home runs for the Orioles one season and became an All-Star outfielder. The interviewer asked him what happened. What motivated him to grow from an average and anonymous player into an All-Star?

Brady said that one day he simply decided he wanted to be an impact player, not a role player. And once he made that commitment between the ears, Brady began the painstaking process of honing his physical skills by accelerating the clockspeed and intensity of his workouts to maximize the talents he'd been given.

His between-the-ears decision to become an impact player triggered a physical dedication he pursued with tremendous discipline and passion. Anderson got much stronger physically by his workouts and emotionally by his endorphin-driven pursuit of his desire to be better than average.

Never forget Brady's message. Being an impact player in life, family or an organization starts with the conscious decision to become one. The drive, the fuel and the motivation come when your brain and soul make a commitment to your heart. Once you make that decision, have the courage to chase it.

Wall #6:

You're More a Party Vegetable than Party Animal.

Beware of digital cocooning! The recent explosion of computer-dependency is luring too many people into a self-created sphere of self-containment. I call it *digital cocooning*. Digital cocooning creates the very real danger of social withdrawal, diminished physical fitness and unintentional social ostracism.

Thrivers don't hide behind computer screens. Instead, they use them as strategic tools to enable themselves to go off and make even *more* things happen than they otherwise could.

Live in an aquarium, not a cave. People like tropical fish much better than bats.

Wall #7:

You Don't Take Pride in "Not Knowing."

One interesting difference between a Thriver, many Drivers and most Survivors is their differing attitudes about not knowing something. Thrivers admit it easily, are happy to learn, and have no neck-high ego hurdle they have to leap before admitting others know more about something than they. To a Thriver, all new knowledge is good regardless of the source.

Drivers, on the other hand, often are more reactive than proactive and a bit less reluctant to admit they learn *anything*, for example, from someone "below" them.

Survivors often sport more of a "don't care" attitude. The exceptions are those who might be at the Survivor stage now, but have ambitions and don't plan on staying there long.

One secret trap door to tunnel under the walls of the Octagon of Mediocrity is to be proud of what you don't know. Be proud, not embarrassed.

The reason is simple. The more you ask, the more you learn. The more you learn, the more you know. The more you know, the less you don't know. So, be proud of what you don't know. Always be inquisitive. Every night, go to bed smarter than you were when you got up that morning.

Learn as much as you can (whenever you can) about anything related to the achievement of your personal Daily Dozen.

Wall #8: *You Are Who You Hang Out With.*

Look around. Assess the people you associate and work with. You are your own peer group. If you aspire for more, change your habits, locales, interests and venues. If you want to learn more, hang out with people who know more than you do.

Beyond the Octagon

While the Octagon encircles a lot of people, there are other subtle differences between Thrivers and lower-level performers.

For example, Thrivers give direct answers to direct questions. They also reflexively ask lots of non-direct questions to learn more or help accumulate information and knowledge.

Thrivers speak directly, speak to be understood, and since they don't fear the truth, they rarely resort to doublespeak or evasive answers when responding to direct, specific questions. And maybe most importantly of all – they *listen*. They learn by listening, not talking.

I also believe that high performers – compared to others – have a much smaller gap between what they *think* they know and what they *really do*. Skilled talents often have a gap between the two the mere wide of a crack in the sidewalk. To others, the gap can be as wide as the fat part of the Grand Canyon.

The better you are at self-assessment, the smaller the gap you're likely to have.

Also, Thrivers *must* read. They are compelled to read. The wider their horizontal fields of learning, the smarter and more conversant they become. Libraries and bookstores are Cathedrals of Joy for those who read – or Temples of Joy, depending on your point of view. Well-read people never stop learning and growing.

Challenge yourself, consciously, to learn daily. Make *learning* part of your own personal brand.

The Octagon of Mediocrity will not expand as your talents do. The Octagon is simply a box that surrounds people of finite talent and ambition. It is, for many, an invisible corral. Fortunately, your talents can outgrow the box's ability to contain you.

On Failure

Thrivers realize that they cannot invent or innovate if they are unwilling to fail. And the better they learn to deal with (and learn from) failure, the better off they'll be.

Failure can be a great coach and teacher, if you let it. Remember the three specific barriers to performance and if you study *why* you were unsuccessful at something, chances are you'll be able to devise future strategies to minimize the chances of losing the same way twice.

Many top performers make just as many – or more – mistakes than others. And they *should* make the most since they make the most things happen.

But Thrivers don't dwell on mistakes. They learn, retain the positives, jettison the negatives, treat it as a learning lesson and move on. They aren't happy being average and won't stand for staying trapped inside The Octagon or wasting time running laps on the Hamster Wheel to Nowhere.

The late actor Jack Lemmon once said, "Failure never hurt anybody. It's the fear of failure that kills you, that kills artists. You've got to go down that alley and take those chances."

Fear of failure can douse talent and smolder, then smother, motivation. Baseball star Reggie Jackson struck out the equivalent of 5½ full baseball seasons – yet *he's* a Hall of Famer. Catfish Hunter, who pitched for five World Series championship teams, called Reggie the best big-game player he ever saw. The reason was simple: When it mattered most, Reggie rose to the occasion, focused on performing rather than fearing failure, and exuded so much radiant confidence his teammates felt more confident, too.

Reggie loved the pressure. Pressure makes diamonds and pressure bursts pipes, but Reggie Jackson truly believed he had earned the right to stand there, under that spotlight, at that time, with everything on the line. Reggie believed he'd earned the right for the pressure to make him a diamond. And, ever-brimming with confidence, Reggie delivered when it mattered most. Reggie continually demonstrated the Attributes of a winner.

Remember: Many of the significant things truly worth attempting in life are difficult. If they weren't, everyone could do them. But there's a heck of a big difference between failing a few times and being a failure. Thrivers might fail en route to succeeding, but the Octagon of Mediocrity can't hold them. And they never – *ever* – doubt their own ability to reach their goals.

Once you decide to be an impact player, not a role player, and a Thriver – not Survivor – your thoughts shift away from aimless unreachable dreams and focus toward higher standards that are measurable, achievable, and worth pursuing.

The Walls of Mediocrity simply cannot hold someone truly determined to succeed.

Few ever *want* to fail. Emerson said, "Every man (and woman) believes that he (or she) has a greater possibility."

Who's to argue?

All of us go to school – some simply stop before others – but what people learn in school is *never* truly measured in letters or numbers. Or fancy titles on business cards. Or bank accounts or stock portfolios. What people learn in school is really measured by what they accomplish afterward and, more importantly, how they go about pursuing their dreams, once they're self-propelling their way through life.

Motivated people will not be confined inside the Walls of Mediocrity, even if those very same walls are tall enough to hold their peers. Motivated people pole vault over, burrow under, or drill though the containment walls. One way or another, they bust out.

A writer more skilled than I once wrote, *"What a person achieves in life is not as important as the obstacles they overcame to achieve it."*

That writer was Booker T. Washington, in his book "Up From Slavery." Booker wrote it a hundred years ago. If everyone who had the desire to better themselves also had the opportunity, the world would be a much, much better place simply because there would be a lot more Thrivers in it.

You can start from any point in your life to move forward and quickly make progress. And once you make that conscious decision to do so, you *will* have a better life.

Greatness is gender-blind and colorblind – a pair of elegant truisms that will forever stand the tests of time. Now – *more than ever* – it's vital to take ownership of your future. And if you do, these walls (and others like them) will _never_ be able to hold you.

Hop over them or climb under them, but leave the Octagon of Mediocrity behind and wave goodbye as you watch it disappear in your rear view mirror.

Chapter 11

Big Ears & Lofty Dreams
Walt, J.K. & The Sands of Possibility

◆

*"You can dream, create, design, and build
the most wonderful place in the world,
but it requires <u>people</u> to make the dream a reality."*
-- Walt Disney

◆

*"I prayed that I would just make enough money
to justify continuing to write."*
-- J.K. Rowling, Scottish author of "Harry Potter."

Walt Disney was born to Flora and Elias Disney on December 5, 1901 at 1249 Tripp Avenue in Chicago. He was named after a family friend, Reverend Walter Parr.

As a teenager Walt Disney worked for his father's newspaper. Walt didn't have a lot of new ideas, things didn't work out and he left to go dabble in art. Art didn't work out so well, either. In just a couple years, his first company went under. It officially sank in July of 1923 when Walt was 21.

Like any persistent Thriver would, Walt shrugged off both work disasters as merely temporary inconveniences. Forced to move into a room of his Uncle Robert's house in Los Angeles, Walt kept persevering. He was convinced there was a market for humorous entertainment shorts in a motion picture format. Determinedly, Disney kept trying to make and sell them.

Few around Walt shared the same conviction. But onward he persevered.

Disney pursued his future with confidence, vision and belief. He envisioned funny cartoon characters and drew them; believed in creating animated short features and made them; and heard the audiences laughing long before they ever saw even his first film.

Great love and great achievement both sometimes involve a significant amount of risk and through his early ups and downs, Walt measured, minimized and studied the downside possibilities connected with trying to realize his dream. He was very much a calculated risk-taker – willing to take a gamble to realize profits, both tangible and intangible.

Walt was roughly two-fifths of the way through his life when he first filed Mickey Mouse trademark protection June 11, 1929. Only 27 at the time, Disney reportedly thought up his mouse concept 15 months before, during a five-day train ride from New York to Los Angeles. He was 26 and close to broke.

Two decades after that train ride, Walt imagined Disneyland fully-finished in his own mind – long before it began to rise from the rural dust and dirt of 165 agrarian Anaheim acres.

And 26 years after thinking up Mickey Mouse during a train ride, Disney's vision, confidence, and hard work forever changed American ideals, parenting and child-rearing.

He opened Disneyland.

The welcoming gates to Disneyland flung open relatively late in Walt's life. He was 53 when the brand new, long-awaited $17 million entertainment complex finally opened on July 17, 1955. It was 32 years after his first company went under.

An invitation-only crowd of 15,000 was invited to the private opening. Nearly twice that many – over 28,000 – showed up and swarmed the park.

The following day, the general public was welcomed. Admission was $1 and the various rides and attractions cost between 10-cents and 35-cents apiece.

Disney lived long enough to see his biggest dream realized, but not its eventual flabbergasting and spinoff successes maximized.

Like Disney, people with a passion for how they live their life each day live with a sense of grateful urgency. They have to. Seeing, doing and achieving what you want in life must be accomplished inside an ever-dwindling window of remaining time.

Disney died from lung cancer December 15, 1966 at 65, seven years shy of the average American male. He ended up living about 2,500 fewer days than the norm but wasted very, very few. His days were shortchanged a bit, by about 10-percent, but he made the most of every moment he was given.

Disney made a difference. Disney had a dream and chased it like a kid after a rainbow. In some ways, Walt was lucky – he caught that rainbow and found his pot of gold. But because he never gave up on what he truly believed in, Walt Disney made a positive impact on hundreds of millions of people.

Another Fateful Train Ride

Less than 20 weeks before Disney's passing, a baby girl named Joanne Kathleen Rowling was born across the Atlantic in Bristol, England. Her life into early adulthood proved a bit of a struggle. But, like Disney 62 years before, J.K. Rowling's life changed during a four-hour 1990 summertime train ride from Manchester to London. She was 24 at the time.

During that train ride, Ms. Rowling envisioned virtually the entire wide-spanning set of stories before she wrote even the first syllable about Harry Potter. J.K. clearly saw the primary characters, particularly Harry, and had the entire series of stories clearly in mind by the time the train docked at King's Cross Station.

None of it had been between her ears when the train shoved off from Manchester four hours before.

But all Jo Rowling had when she climbed up and out of that London train station was a story, a baby, and a flicker of optimism. What she didn't have was an agent, a book deal, a husband or two dimes to rub together. A nasty divorce had taken care of the latter two.

She abandoned two adult novels she'd been working on, choosing instead to focus on writing a children's book she probably couldn't sell.

In many ways, Rowling's was a very similar situation to what Walt Disney went through – although the two starmakers lived three generations and one big ocean apart.

J.K. didn't have any money when she thought up Harry Potter. Like Disney, J.K's riches were still between the ears and not in the bank. *That* has since been remedied. Her last advance was, I believe, $10 million. Her fortune grows daily.

Both these train-envisioned imaginary characters – Mickey Mouse and Harry Potter – are now known all over the world.

"It is hard to be defined by the most difficult part of your life," Ms. Rowling said about her struggles to raise the baby, finish the book, and find a publisher who cared. Several publishing houses immediately rejected "Harry Potter." She kept persevering.

The agent who finally agreed to take on Rowling's project was a man she'd contacted because she liked the sound of his name – Christopher Little. Little sold Rowling's story to a British company that specialized in children's books.

"I prayed that I would make just enough money to justify continuing to write," Rowling said, "because I am supporting my daughter single-handedly."

Even after the book was sold, J. K. planned on giving French lessons to help make ends meet.

"Harry Potter" quickly grew legs, gained rapid popularity throughout Great Britain, and it soon became obvious the story had a chance to be a success in the United States. The U.S. rights went up for auction. Ms. Rowling was flabbergasted at what the book rights sold for. Suddenly, she was set for life. Literally overnight, speaking French became something she'd have to do only if she ever decided she felt like it.

Much of the story J. K. envisioned on the train that day was fabricated. One key aspect wasn't.

"I think the only event in my own life that changed the direction of "Harry Potter" was the death of my mother," she said. "I only realized upon re-reading the book how many of my own feelings about losing my mother I had given Harry."

This revealing point – that a significant emotional event strongly influenced the life of one of the world's most popular writers and also her famous book's principle character – is a key message we will return to in a following chapter.

Significant emotional events play a critical role in all our lives. They shape and re-shape who we are, what we think and what our values are.

And a critically significant emotional event in J. K. Rowling's life helped shape the magic of the character that keyed the global popularity of the series. "Harry Potter" is now sold worldwide in approximately 30 languages.

Ms. Rowling still lives in Edinburgh, raising daughter Jessica and churning out pages toward the completion of the seven-book series she envisioned so clearly the day she rode the train to London. When she's finally finished telling Harry's story, she'll have spent 13 years writing about a little wizard. She has no similar expectations on future success beyond Harry.

"I've been (writing) all my life and it is necessary to me," she said about her future. "I don't feel quite normal if I haven't written for awhile.

"I doubt I will ever again write anything as popular as the "Harry" books, but I can live with that thought quite easily."

Admiring the phenomenal success of Ms. Rowling's personal story is easy. After a bitter divorce left her with little but a baby and her own ability, she had the confidence to pursue her dreams

185

and invested every spare moment in two things she steadfastly believed in. One was the story she had to tell. The other was her ability to tell it.

It paid off. Jo Rowling hit the jackpot. But the key messages are that she *earned the right* to have something good happen and zealously followed a passion. J. K. had the knowledge (she knew what she needed to write about), the skills to write it well, and the attributes to focus on bulldoggedly finishing the story and finding someone else who shared her passion for the work she'd created.

Rowling made her own luck possible. Great fortune requires good luck sometimes, but Ms. Rowling's hard work and faith in her story and herself paid off. All the countless hours of writing in fragments whenever and wherever her baby daughter fell asleep – be it a local café, the laundromat or her tiny dark apartment – individually seemed inconsequential. Yet, when added together, they delivered an extraordinary success story to the busy old streets of Edinburgh.

Fair and square, Jo Rowling earned her great success.

Time and passion were everything to Rowling, as they were to Disney. Each treated time they way everyone should treat it – like a precious, irreplaceable resource. There are but four true ways to while away your hours and that's what we'll talk about next.

The Four Ways to Spend Your Day

Regardless of how many days you life's allocation contains, there are really only four ways that time will elapse. You can either:

1. *CHERISH IT.*

2. *INVEST IT.*

3. *SPEND IT; or*

4. *WASTE IT.*

186

1. Cherish Time

Time you cherish is tied to the heart. Lifelong memories are created and you live in the moment, for the moment. The clock means nothing.

Cherish Time is the easiest of the four time utilization categories to identify. It's also the rarest, since these are the special minutes, moments, hours and experiences that form the cornerstone memories of your life. Cherish Time comes in those special occasions when you feel most wonderfully alive.

Events that mean the most to us are singularly individualistic. For many, these are private moments with a growing child or intimate partner. Has any parent ever forgotten a child's first steps or first wobbly ride on a bicycle? Or watching that same child leave home for college or drive off to a new job in a distant town?

For others, Cherish Time surrounds more innately personal emotions stemming from the individual achievement of pursuing, then attaining, a long-desired or lifelong goal. Often they're influenced by emotional experiences of the past. Every marathon finisher is flooded with emotion when they cross the finish line and realize they've achieved something in life they never thought they could.

Watching a small child land a big fish can deliver the same warm set of feelings. There are thousands of wonderful ways to capture the magic emotions of life at its most precious and freeze-framed best.

Cherish Time is richly fulfilling and memorable. These special events stash a bit of life equity into your soul and are the special overpowering moments that make life worth living – the brief cresting peaks of life's rumbling roller-coaster.

Cherish Time yields the defining and most memorable moments of your life and there's no rule that says you can't have a whole lot of them. Try hard to consciously make them a part of every day – or as many days as possible.

Think back to your very own. What are they? What made them so very special that you refuse to ever let them go? How can you repeat them? Or build on them? Better still, what can *you* do to create new ones?

Early in the book we talk about being rich without money and how important it is to embrace the importance of that philosophy as it relates to being content and happy on The Pro Leisure Tour.

Well, the richest and most contented folks of all are those with the largest amounts of Cherish Time safely stashed in the memory bank.

2. *Investment Time*

Happy and productive people typically route a lot of time toward the necessary pieces of the puzzles they're trying to complete. *Investment Time* comes from building equity in others (and you). Education is an investment. Support is an investment. Reading, researching and chasing new knowledge all are investments.

Time spent with children and loved ones are investments too. So are pursuing hobbies that bring you pleasure. Personally, I love the creation process of writing – developing ideas, picking the right words and their best order to deliver the thought or idea I want to convey.

I also consider the time I flyfish in the mountains for trout or stalk bonefish on the shallow-water saltwater flats to be great investments of my time. Both are quiet, soul-enriching beautiful sports where the only inconvenience is an occasional sore lip to an obliging fish – each of which I release to swim another day. My fishing is my guest visit to nature's house. Every minute is precious since the emotionally-recharging solitude is so valuable to me. Some days a wristwatch simply serves no practical value.

All the pieces of life that contribute toward carrying the bricks, carting the blocks and pushing the boulders of life uphill are investments in time – assuming, of course, that all – including

188

the boulder – are parts of the castle of happiness you're constructing atop the mountain. Investment Time is earmarked energy that helps achieve things that eventually help us succeed.

Whereas Cherish Time deals with the heart and soul, Investment Time deals more with the head. For example, the creation of endorphins *always* translates into Investment Time. Endorphins fuel your emotional and physical well-being. Sometimes the creation of those endorphins even helps lift an event or circumstance beyond Investment Time and into the rarefied air of Cherish Time. Fall in love and see what I mean.

Investment Time fuels achievement. Time you *Invest* in yourself – and others – is always repaid, with interest. Same with time Invested in a career path you love pursuing.

Make Investment Time a conscious, growing part of every single day. Thrivers always strive to maximize their daily Investment Time – the more, the better.

Pause for a minute and think about your *own* pursuits.

How do <u>*you*</u> currently invest *your* time? More importantly, how could you improve and invest *more*?

3. Spending Time

When you occupy yourself with things that don't lead toward anything of significant short or long-term value, you are *Spending Time* rather than Investing it.

For most people, Spending Time is generally the largest slice of the four-piece time utilization pie. It's a phenomenon that enables busy people to stay busy without every really becoming productive.

For example, waiting for someone who's habitually late for meetings is a frustrating way to Spend Time since, given another option, you might prefer to do something else.

Spending Time involves two types of things:

189

a) *Things you choose to allocate time to; and,*

b) *Things thrust upon you that require your time. For some, this might even include their job.*

Many of us choose to Spend Time on things that pass the time away but seem to lack any long-term Investment value.

For example, flyfishing time on the river is Investment Time to me, even though I release everything I catch. The actual fishing hours standing in the river waving a stick are an emotional cleansing – an investment.

But the 2-hour drive each way sure isn't. I *Spend* the time to drive out and back because I choose to. I need to spend time to create an important Investment for myself.

Several activities I'm involved with require my time, too. Some stem from the involvement tax of parenthood. Shuttling kids all around town in heavy afternoon traffic is hardly wasted time – but it certainly isn't invested, either. Nope. It's *spent*.

Sometimes, choosing to Spend Time on things you enjoy is valuable simply because you re-charge your batteries and drain some built-up stress like old dirty motor oil from your car's oil pan. If it helps enough, non-taxing activities might even do you enough good to be considered Investment Time. Few people would say they Invest Time at an auto race, golf tournament or baseball or football game. But millions enjoy Spending Time there.

Same with shopping at the mall.

Conversely, forced activities – those thrust upon us – often chew up valuable hours without any redeeming value. Manage these the best you can since they can sneak up from a thousand angles. People at work can lure you into non-efficient uses of your time – especially if it means less work for them. Guard your time like your money. Protect yourself from time robbers.

I've worked with many people over the years who *never* pause to relax. They try to overload so much into a day – especially at

190

work – that they start living a sound-bite existence. Their attention span often shortens, while stress levels increase. Their relentless drive for more and more is circular, not vertical. For them, there is no summit.

But no matter how much more these people attain or acquire, it never seems to be enough. These folks are largely incapable of ever being rich without money unless they smell the coffee and change their current behavior.

People unable to relax are no longer able to see a pine, maple, or oak. All they see is a tree, if they even see it at all – and half the time they don't.

So, stay cognizant of how you're Spending your time. Pick your pursuits for a positive reason, and manage them the best you can.

4. Wasting Time

There are more ways to *Waste Time* than there are jellybeans.

For example, chewing up potential valuable hours watching mindless TV, aimlessly surfing the Internet, or watching a movie for the second or third time eat up lots of hours with little residual hope of ever a producing a payoff.

If you sit back and take a look at people with bad substance abuse habits, it's no wonder they rarely enjoy living their lives to the very best of their ability. Every step of the process involved with those habits eats up time in non-productive ways.

For example, drinking to excess takes time; the period of inebriation takes time; and the resultant shedding of the morning-after hangover takes time. The payoff for the total exercise is a Wasted evening, morning – or both.

People who waste disproportionate amounts of time will achieve less, relative to others.

Doing More:
"The 25ʰ Hour" & How to Find It

Dynamic young business leader William R. McDermott, Executive Vice President of Worldwide Sales for technology giant Siebel Systems, is an outspoken proponent of living every day with a zealous commitment to getting as much done as you possibly can.

McDermott refers to heightened activity levels as *"The 25ᵗʰ Hour."* He urges all his people to find it, then live it. He also urges his people to live a well-balanced life.

McDermott offers five tips on finding the time to cram more into each day:

1. *Set high standards.*

The more you expect of yourself (at home or in the office), the more you will achieve in life. There's a direct and distinct correlation.

2. *Get organized.*

Organization feeds strategic thought. Increased results don't stem from just working smarter, or just working harder. You need to do *both*; and getting organized is the key to the kingdom.

3. *Do your homework.*

The more you know, the more you increase your chances of success. Lazy people cut corners. Achievers don't. They know that homework research is always time very well-invested.

4. *Execute flawlessly.*

Success blossoms from the methodical planting, fertilization, watering, pruning and harvesting of ideas and goals worth nurturing. Practice and preparation build the confidence that helps shape smooth execution. Things done right the first time rarely need to be done over a second time. That holds true in business, and it holds true at home.

5. *Stay in shape.*

McDermott refers here to both physical and cerebral conditioning. It's impossible to perform your best, day-after-day, if you're not firing on all cylinders.

How to Live that 25th Hour

Those previous five tips are McDermott's suggestions for finding that elusive 25th Hour. Once that hour is found, he's got five more tips for how to effectively live it:

1. *Take care of home base.*

Your home, along with the people in it, is the single most important place in your life. Live this urgency within its walls and treat your family far beyond how you treat yourself.

2. *Perpetual optimism.*

Be a *"how-can-we"* person. Never think *"can't because."* Optimists achieve more than pessimists. Carve it in stone.

3. *Change minds, champion the cause.*

Achievers are leaders. There are more followers than leaders in the world and the world needs more leaders.

4. *Lead and teach.*

Leading is one thing – but *teaching* while you're leading is how everyone around you gets more done, too. Leaders and teachers are impact players, not role players. Be an impact player.

5. *Have an unbreakable spirit.*

Busy people make things happen. When things happen, some go well and some don't. Continually demonstrate a zest and zeal for living. When that attitude becomes part of the very backbone of who you are, you'll have a magnetic personality trait people will always admire.

McDermott's advice certainly works. Prior to joining Siebel, he joined Xerox Corporation after college and within a decade was the youngest corporate officer in the company. A dynamic leader by example, McDermott continually urges all his people to do one more thing each day, one *extra* thing, in the organized and well-defined pursuit of that elusive 25th Hour.

It's sage advice and well worth taking.

A Topic Summary: *"Be Better, Not Perfect."*

So, how have you used *your* hours today? Glance back at what occupied your time since the day began at midnight. We don't all build Disney Worlds or write runaway bestsellers – but we all *can* take the time to study what we've done with the time we've been given and maximize the positive things we do for our family and ourselves.

A sample chart is on a following page. On it you can write a quick list of what you did today and how long you spent on each activity.

Next, decide *how* the time that ticked away during each of those activities elapsed. Select what category each fell into. Rate each activity independently of the others.

Once you've made your category determinations, total up (in hours and minutes) how your day went in each of the four time-use categories: *Cherish, Invest, Spend,* and *Waste.*

Those totals tell you what you did with your day – how large and small you sliced the four pieces of your daily pie. If the Waste piece is the biggest, set out tomorrow to make it smaller. And the day after that, make it smaller again.

We are all very much creatures of habit. Most of us live in very well-defined patterns and routines that can be very hard to break. *How* we each use our hours is very likely to be habit-formed and molded. So, when you decide to change those habits, be wary of one very important consideration: *There is a very high probability those habits will fight you!* Be prepared for that and expect it.

The end-goal connected to guarding your time and wisely choosing how you use it is simple: *We want to be better, not perfect.*

Perfect is too hard. Everyone who's ever tried to be has failed. But being *better* about slicing bigger pieces of the time pie for things we Cherish and want to Invest in is absolutely attainable for all of us.

The more we accomplish in life in the manner in which we expect it to be done, the more fulfilling each day becomes.

Commit to create as much achievement, investment and fulfillment as you possibly can and keep that unbreakable spirit. The internal confidence you generate will become as much a part of what fuels your life as breakfast, lunch and dinner.

Investing your time to live your Daily Dozen is a free ticket to a contented life on the PLT. Remember: *"Live life, love the journey . . . . and make things happen!"*

(see chart on following page)

How Do *You* Use an Average Day?

HOUR	Activity	HOW USED	HOUR	ACTIVITY	HOW USED
to 1 a.m.	Sleep	Invested	1 p.m.	Work	Wasted
2 a.m.	Sleep	Invested	2 p.m.	Work	(*you* decide)*
3 a.m.	Sleep	Invested	3 p.m.	Work	(*you* decide)*
4 a.m.	Sleep	Invested	4 p.m.	Work	(*you* decide)*
5 a.m.	Sleep	Invested	5 p.m.	Commute	Wasted
6 a.m.	Sleep	Invested	6 p.m.	Exercise	Invested
7 a.m.	Dress & Commute	Spent	7 p.m.	Relax and Read	Invested
8 a.m.	Work	(*you* decide)*	8 p.m.	Read	Invested
9 a.m.	Work	(*you* decide)*	9 p.m.	Watch TV	Spent
10 a.m.	Work	(*you* decide)*	10 p.m.	Intimacy	Cherish
11 a.m.	Work	Wasted	11 p.m.	Sleep	Invested
noon	Lunch	Spent	Midnight	Sleep	Invested
A.M totals:	Cherish Invested Spent Wasted *TBD* (work?)*	0 hours 6 hours 2 hours 1 hours 3 hours	P.M. totals:	Cherish Invested Spent *Wasted* ** *TBD* (work?)*	1 hour 5 hours 1 hour 2 hour 3 hours

* -- How "Work" is measured is totally up to you. To some people, it's *Wasted* time. To others it's *Spent*. Ideally, you'd like it *Invested*. To a scant lucky few, it's *Cherished*.

Note from the chart that "commuting time" isn't always *Wasted*. When possible, many people use the time effectively for personal enrichment of various sorts: Reading, listening to audiobooks, planning their day and various other helpful things.

Note, too, that in this charted example, for the sake of illustration the worker kills the hour before lunch and the one immediately after doing nothing of value.

Once you've determined your daily allocations and totaled them all up, it's pretty simple to create a pie chart to illustrate how you presently use your time.

For example, in the charted illustration on the previous page, let's assume that the non-wasted Work Hours are of a value *"To Be Determined."*

If that's the case, the 24-hour day synopsizes like this:

◆	# of hours Wasted:	3 of 24 =	12.5 %
◆	# of hours Spent:	3 of 24 =	12.5 %
◆	# of hours Invested: (if sleep is an investment)	11 of 24 =	45.8 %
◆	# of hours Cherished	1 of 24 =	4.2 %
◆	# of hours TBD (work)	6 of 24 =	25.0 %
	Daily Totals	**24 Hours =**	**100 %**

It's obvious that a critical factor concerning the relative value of your day is how you feel about what you do for a living. **Work attitude plays a *massive* role in how we view our lives and the quality of life we're living.**

You, of course, are the final judge for what category all these time occupiers belong in. But what is pretty much indisputable is the knowledge that the quality of the life you're living is largely dependent upon how big a time slice you can cut yourself for the Cherish category, and how big a slice you cut for Invested Time. Those two categories are far and away the most important.

The bigger *they* are, the happier you'll be.

Time Utilization Breakdown

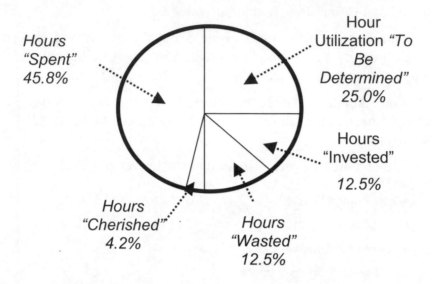

Hours
"Spent"
45.8%

Hour
Utilization *"To
Be
Determined"*
25.0%

Hours
"Invested"
12.5%

Hours
"Cherished"
4.2%

Hours
"Wasted"
12.5%

The Dramatic Impact of Enjoying Your Work

In the pie chart example above, we've determined that one-fourth of our day (our non-wasted work hours) is in the category *"To Be Determined."* The chart below summarizes the impact that loving, liking and not-liking your work can have on the quality of life you're living.

For the sake of the exercise, let's assume if someone *Cherishes* their work or considers it *Invested Time*, they won't waste any hours during the day.

If they consider their job *Spent Time*, they'll fritter away one (1) hour a day. If they don't like their work at all, and consider it *Wasted Time,* let's assume two (2) non-productive hours a day.

The following two charts illustrate the dramatic power that work can have on how you perceive the quality of your life:

24 HOURS PER DAY
(if sleep is "Invested" Time)

If Work Hours are:	# Waste Hours Daily	# Spent Hours Daily	# Invested Hours Daily	# Cherished Hours Daily	Total # of Daily Hours (incl. sleep)	Total # of Hours *Invested* & *Cherished*
Cherished	1	3	11	9	24	20 of 24 83.3%
Invested	1	3	19	1	24	20 of 24 83.3%
Spent	2	10	11	1	24	12 of 24 50%
Wasted	9	3	11	1	24	12 of 24 50%

WAKING HOURS ONLY

If Work Hours are:	Daily Hours Wasted	Daily Hrs Spent	Daily Hours Invested	Daily Hours. Cherished	Total # of Waking Hours	# of Hours *Invested* & *Cherished*
Cherished	1	3	3	9	16	12 of 16 75%
Invested	1	3	11	1	16	12 of 16 75%
Spent	2	10	3	1	16	4 of 16 25%
Wasted	9	3	3	1	16	4 of 16 25%

The Impact of Removing Sleep from the Quality of Life Equation

Once the value of sleep is parked to the side, the dramatic impact that job satisfaction can have on personal fulfillment becomes startlingly apparent. Clearly it will have a huge impact on how you see your life.

The message, then, is clear: You *must* have a sense of urgency concerning how the grains of sand in your life tumble en route from the top of your hourglass to the bottom. And that same sense of urgency must apply to keeping yourself occupied during waking hours with things you really enjoy doing – whether you get paid for them or not.

When you track your time for awhile, the pie slices of your lifestyle will take on more of a consistently measured size. Try it for a typical week or two and see what happens. Patterns will develop. When they do, remember your objective: *Increase* the slices of Cherish and Investment Time, and *decrease* the slices of Spent and Wasted Time.

If you're happy and content with the life you're living, then your time utilization mix might be just about perfect.

But if you'd like to be happier more often, or increase the amount of inner peace and contentment you feel, then assess how your daily activities currently slice up your personal time pie and make a conscious decision to change the size of those slices.

Changing the size of the slices will require changing habits and old habits fight back. The older and more ingrained the habit, the harder it probably will be to shed.

Shed it anyway.

As simple as it sounds, few people ever step back to think about how they analytically allocate their time. Even fewer lay it out on paper and study it with a determined eye on time utilization improvement.

Your attitude toward what you do for a living obviously has a huge impact on the size of the pie slices you cut.

Remember that there is, of course, a big very difference between being busy and being happy. There are a lot of very busy and hugely unhappy people out there – way too many. People can be very busy and yet achieve very little of redeeming value. But to a large extent, we all have choices inside each and every day and those choices dictate how we occupy our preciously limited and valuable waking hours.

Your life, in the end, will be scripted based on the time utilization choices you've made along the way.

Summary

How our time is used each day is sliced into four different-size slices of our own personal time-utilization pie.

1. One wedge is the time we use doing something we *Cherish*.

2. Another slice is the amount of time we've *Invested* in pursuit of good-value goals.

3. The third is how many hours and minutes were simply *Spent* treading water without a fulfilling reward.

4. And fourth is the amount of life in a day that's simply *Wasted*.

The challenge for all of us is to determine the best achievable balance for the life we're happiest to lead. Our Daily Dozen helped define what that life would be. It's up to us to allocate our time the best we can to achieve those 12 important ambitions.

Stay cognizant of the four categories and repeatedly challenge yourself to allocate and steer your time wisely into the specific categories you want your life most fulfillingly comprised of.

Cherish Activities:

Precious time is always good for the soul. Special moments and unforgettable memories shape the greatest times of our life. Time slows in anticipation; flies upon arrival. Consciously make cherish moments, at a minimum, a sliver of every single day for the rest of your life.

Invest Activities:

Examples include activities to feed the brain, physical fitness, strategic planning, research, and prudent moves based on the pursuit of longer-term personal and professional goals. Plan to cut yourself a great big slice of *Investment* pie every single morning.

Spend Activities:

Always try and *Spend* your time on activities *you* choose. Avoid being a dumping-ground for the time-robbing chores of others. Spend time on what *you* want each day, and always try to squeeze out some positives. When you Spend time on things, try and figure out a way to turn that Spending Time into *Investment Time*.

Waste Activities:

Avoid time-eaters that could have been eliminated with the hours better spent in one of the other three categories rather than tossed away. *If you do nothing else except consciously shrink the size of this slice, you automatically must grow at least one of the other three.*

Many of these time robbers wear shoes, so guard against them and push back! If you do, you can't *help* but live a more efficient and fulfilling day than you did before.

Wasting time is largely controllable and dominated by bad habits. Replace those bad habits with an investment in time for something that interests you. You'll see quick dividends and, over time, you'll be paid back handsomely.

202

"Time Is Money"

What Your Time is Worth — in $$$$$ & Cents

Another way to heighten your sense of urgency concerning how to use each day is to understand what your time truly *is* worth. Once you realize, in dollars and cents, what your time really *is* worth, chances are you'll quit wasting as much of it.

People sling that phrase around like an airborne frisbee: *"Time is money!"*

It sure is. Next time you hear it, ask the speaker what theirs is worth. There's little chance they'll know.

People *should* know what their time is worth. Shown on the next page is a simple chart that breaks down annual income levels into easily measurable dollars-per-hour. The assumption is simple: What you earn per hour at work is what your time is worth.

Remember: Time is your most valuable asset – and it is, and always will be – irreplaceable. Use it accordingly and keep that in mind as you study the following.

The Chart Assumes:

♦ A standard 40-hour work week and 50-week-per-year job responsibility – creating a 2,000-hour annual workload.

♦ Income levels between $30,000 and $200,000 per year.

♦ The *earnings-per-hour* are how much – in dollars and cents – is earned based on annual income divided by the expected 2,000 work hours per year (50 weeks X 40 hours per week).

♦ Located on the page following the chart is a simple formula to enable you to quickly calculate your own. With the formula is an easy-to-use reference table for the ever-growing number of people who work *more* than 40 hours a week.

For the adventurous (and curious), feel free to adjust this dollars-per-hour logic to include variables like subtracting the amount of work hours wasted each year *(which lets you figure out*

203

your <u>true</u> earnings-per-work-hour).   Then, figure out how much more money you'd earn if you truly worked all the hours that were frittered away.

As a manager, I always wanted my salespeople to know *exactly* what their time was worth.   A roomful of people who know what an internal meeting is costing them has a much higher level of expectation than a roomful who doesn't.

(see chart on following page)

What Your Time is *Truly* Worth

Dollar ($) Earnings per Year	Hours Worked per Year	Average $$ Earnings per Hour **"What Your Time is Truly Worth"**
$ 5,000	2,000	$ 2.50 per hour
30,000	2,000	15.00
40.000	2,000	20.00
50,000	2,000	25.00
60,000	2,000	30.00
70,000	2,000	35.00
80,000	2,000	40.00
90,000	2,000	45.00
100,000	2,000	50.00
125,000	2,000	62.50
150,000	2,000	75.00
200,000	2,000	100.00

note: The $5,000 hourly rate can be added to the other income levels to help interpolate additional income level calculations.

What happens if you are among the unfortunate millions working in excess of 40 hours per week? Check the formula and chart on the next page to quickly figure out how much *YOUR* earnings per hour truly are.

Calculate Your Own Value per Hour:

$$\$\underline{\hspace{3cm}} \div \underline{\hspace{3cm}} = \$\underline{\hspace{2cm}}$$

(Annual $ Earnings) ÷ (# of Hrs Worked Per Yr)   = *Your* $ per *hour.*

A lot of people work a heck of a lot more than 40 hours a week!   If you're one of them, select the appropriate number of hours you work each year from the chart below and enter it into the simple formula above.

Then do the math. Everyone should know what their true time is worth. Remember: There are only 168 hours, total, in a week.

Annual Hours Worked Chart
(40+ hours per week)

	48 weeks *(4 weeks annual vacation)*	49 weeks *(3 weeks annual vacation)*	50 weeks (2 weeks annual vacation)
40 hrs/week	1,920	1,960	2,000
45 hrs/week	2,160	2,205	2,250
50 hrs/week	2,400	2,450	2,500
55 hrs/week	2,640	2,695	2,750
60 hrs/week	2,880	2,940	3,000
65 hrs/week	3,120	3,185	3,250
70 hrs/week	3,360	3,430	3,500
80 hrs/week	3,840	3,920	4,000
90 hrs/week	4,320	4,410	4,500

Chapter 12

Making the Impossible Possible
How to "See the End & Work Backward"

Once mastered, the simple techniques of this chapter will dramatically improve your life at home and in the office!

Treat this powerful technique with the respect of an elephant. Master this skill and you, too, will cross the seemingly impossible Alps of achievement.

This chapter is all about learning *how* to achieve more – quickly and efficiently – with minimal wasted time. It will give a big boost toward helping you live your personal and professional life in the most productive and effective ways possible.

This chapter teaches you how to *"See the End & Work Backward."* You will learn how to envision a goal and, starting from today, accurately road-map the distance between where you are and where you want to go.

Its true power, beautifully enough, is that this is a life skill and its effectiveness applies interchangeably at home and work. Once you learn to think this way, its application will pay off in a thousand benefits throughout the rest of your life.

Few people argue the ability to *"See the End & Work Backward"* is a great concept and wonderful strategy. But fewer still are the people who know how. *You* are about to learn.

"Seeing The End & Working Backward" is a learned skill, not a born one. It's another one of those important things that college should teach – but doesn't. And once you learn and master this technique, I hope you'll take the time to teach and mentor others to learn it, too.

The Scourge of the "Two-Puzzlers"

A dozen years or so ago I was headed to a staff meeting at the Xerox International Training Center with an old whitehaired gentleman named Emmett Reagan. Emmett was in his mid-60s and negotiating his final year before retirement. Still, he showed up religiously for every staff meeting with a fresh pad of notebook paper and a just-sharpened pencil.

Although Emmett always sat to the side of the room, about halfway back, whenever I looked over at him he was studiously taking notes, pausing throughout each module to carefully write on his pad.

I could never figure out what the heck Emmett thought was so important since half the time these meetings had no apparent purpose other than to allow us all to get paid while watching the hands of the wall clock go round-and-round in excruciatingly slow motion.

One day we both approached the meeting room from opposite ends of a long hallway. After changing brief guttural grunts of salutation (a typical male greeting), Emmett looked at me and said, "I got a funny feelin' this one's gonna be a Two-Puzzler."

I quizzically furrowed a brow and had to ask for clarification. "What's a Two-Puzzler, Em?"

He looked at me and laughed loudly with his deep-Virginia baritone laugh. "A Two-Puzzler's a meeting where you got plenty of time to finish two of *these*," he said, flipping up the top sheet of his yellow legal pad.

There rested two carefully folded New York Times crossword puzzles.

Turns out that Emmett hadn't taken but a handful of notes in the 15 years he'd been there. But thanks to the relentless blizzard of meetings he'd been forced to sit through, Emmett finished *hundreds* of puzzles. And they are hard puzzles.

Efficient meetings are tightly run according to a schedule of pre-determined, agenda-listed objectives. Inefficient meetings aren't. Inefficiently-run meetings waste beaches full of valuable sand granules all across the country every single day.

That time wasted can never be recovered. Busy people know this and it's why they detest the majority of meetings they're forced to attend. Thrivers perceive them to be high cost, low-return uses of their time. Bad meetings shrink the size of Investment Time and Cherish Time slices in everyone's daily pie.

That lost down-the-drain time is valuable in economic terms, too. Earlier, we saw *exactly how valuable* in dollars and cents. When people *know* what their time is worth, they push back much more quickly against tolerating time-wasting activities. They grow *out of* the habit of accepting time wasters, and *into* a habit that rejects them.

People who can "See The End" don't waste time. They cut to the chase because the focus of what they do in life changes from where they are to where they want to end up. They latch onto that end-vision and stay focused on it with both eyes.

In order to *"See The End & Work Backward"* you have to know specifically what you want to accomplish – the precise end-result you want to achieve. Once you define that specific goal – you retreat, and think about all the necessary steps that must be taken in order to moonwalk backward from the end vision all the way to the present state.

On the following pages are easy step-by-step ways to do just that.

Neatly, logically and with an artful simplicity, by the end of this chapter you will have learned how to think differently and become much more efficient at anything you choose to achieve.

This new thought approach fits like a fur-lined glove over both the left hand of your personal life and the right hand of your business life. It's a "how can we" problem solving approach to creative thought rather than a tactic-laced formula that says "do this and say this." Once you learn to think this way, the ability to "See the End & Work Backward" becomes automatic.

An important message concerning adult learning is well-worth mentioning since it helps underscore the learning process involved with mastering this valuable skill. I learned this at Xerox and it's proven to be tremendously helpful ever since.

When it comes to learning new skills, adults go through four distinct stages of learning:

1. First, we're "*Unconsciously Incompetent*."

At the onset of a new learning experience, we are simply *unaware* that we are incapable of doing something the way it needs to be done.

Until the very first time you step in a whitewater raft and float bouncing and zooming down the Arkansas River during spring run-off, you never realize *how much* there is to know about something you know so very little about.

No beginning rafter has the Knowledge, Skills, or Attributes to survive a whitewater blast through Brown's Canyon. And that's the reasons no beginners are allowed to try and go through it without a guide.

2. Next, we become "*Consciously Incompetent*."

Awareness quickly sets in. We don't know what we need to know, but now at least realize it. We also own the realization that what we need to learn is very much worth the effort.

On a first-time float down the Arkansas, this realization generally dawns on raft occupants at the first ominous hydraulic wall of churning, foaming water – about 100 yards into the trip.

3. Third, after some training and practice, we become "*Consciously Competent*."

In other words, if we pay attention, do things right and maybe refer to our instructions, we can achieve the desired result. Doing everything isn't automatic yet but at least we've experienced success and understand the necessary success formula.

Learning proper paddling technique, following the orders of your guide and executing flawlessly to help steer the rocketing raft safely around the most treacherous whitewater boulders is a good example of Conscious Competence.

4. Finally, we reach the stage of learning and effectiveness we want. We reach a stage of *"Unconscious Competence."*

At this stage, the necessary success steps are ingrained and pretty much automatic. You can perform them successfully without help and almost without thinking. Every step you need to take in order to succeed becomes as automatic as tying your shoelaces or brushing your teeth.

The rafting guides, for example, are *Unconsciously Competent*. They have all the required Knowledge, Skills and Attributes to successfully complete their trips safely. They do not have to think about what they're doing next or why. Everything necessary to succeed is ingrained into their skill sets as professionals.

That, of course, is where we all want to end up when we learning a valuable life skill like "Seeing the End & Working Backward."

Unconsciously Competent is what we want to be, and getting there takes some practice.

A common rule-of-thumb in adult learning is that it often takes 16-to-20 repetitions of a new skill before an adult reaches proficiency.

Some people I've taught this "See the End" technique to have picked it up right away and quickly sailed down the river of building strategic plans on their own. Others bumped into a few rocks. Learning is different for all of us. What matters most is mastering this skill – becoming Unconsciously Competent by whatever means necessary – and using this strategic though approach whenever possible.

Don't expect to leap right into stage four Unconscious Competence the first or second time you use it. If you do, congratulations. Few do. I sure didn't.

7 Success Guidelines

There are seven important points to embrace before we begin with the exercise.

#1: **This technique requires writing things down.**

All three key strategy components will end up being written down: The eventual goal itself, the current state, and the specific steps needed in order to reach that particular goal.

"Less than 3% of the world's population has a *written* goal," said George Simmons. "And I propose to you that until they are written down, they probably won't be achieved."

The "See the End" process is word-dependent, and writing each step down is critical to success. You don't have to write much – very little, actually – but words are important and your ideas and steps will end up being synopsized in concise phrases very much the way your Daily Dozen was crafted.

#2: **Goals must be realistically attainable.**

Being realistically achievable is the difference between a goal and a pipe dream. Pipe dreams are unreachable. A goal is something you *can* accomplish. Lofty goals require tremendous achievement – but they are attainable and the "See the End" strategy was custom-made to help deliver them.

Big fish are always worth fishing for. As a senior in college, I watched a guy catch a big shark off a pier and decided I wanted to do the same. Piece by piece, I spent six or eight weeks assembling the necessary gear. I fished six hours a night, four or five nights a week, for six weeks before I finally got a bite.

That translates to about 150 hours sitting on an upturned bucket, waiting.

The hammerhead shark was 11-feet-long, 650 pounds, and the fight lasted 3½ hours – 'til half past midnight.

The experience of reaching that goal was worth every single dollar and minute I invested in its pursuit – including the hospital time after being gaffed in the leg when we dragged it up on the beach.

I saw the end first – me with a big shark – and worked backward from there. The fish was twice as big as what I'd hoped for but good luck, in life *and* business, sometimes has very long tentacles.

This formula works, so I urge you to use it and apply it to all aspects of your life.

#3: **This is a replicatable way of thinking that helps create plans and achieve goals.**

This process transfers itself equally as effectively to business issues *AND* personal living. It is *a life skill.* Consider it a very helpful "thought reengineering" method that's equally applicable to both personal and professional goal attainment. Regardless of the nature of the challenge, our thought approach will always be the same.

#4: **Every piece of the plan must tie directly and specifically to the achievement of the end goal.**

"See the End" planning involves solving a road map jigsaw puzzle by interlocking every necessary piece snugly into its proper place.

Executing the plan then becomes simply a matter of following your map from where you are to where you want to go. Every piece is critical to arriving at the desired destination.

#5: **Time is of the essence.**

We develop these plans with a sense of urgency and we execute them with an even *greater* sense of urgency. Looking at a plan won't get you anywhere. Pulling it off *will*.

Several times throughout the book we've talked about the great power that comes from working like a Thriver. When you merge your Knowledge, Skills and Attributes with a well-thought out strategic plan to deliver a much-desired result, you are *Investing* every single minute of the plan's development and execution. You are _maximizing_ your efficiency and taking action steps that are all connected in a well-defined straight line and saving great amounts of precious time.

Conversely, if you *don't* have a completed jigsaw puzzle, aimlessly sailing a rudderless boat and hoping something gets done wastes half your time – or maybe even more. You also won't know which shore to aim for since you have no map.

Life on the Pro Leisure Tour means maximizing our results through continual achievement. The easiest way to do that is to Invest and Cherish as much time as we possibly can. The smartest and best way to do that is to apply the "See the End" technique whenever you can. Become unconsciously competent with it and use it often.

For example, if thinking smarter saves you a mere *20 minutes* a day, you save 120 waking hours – over one full waking week – each and every year. In more valuable terms, that's a great opportunity for you to *reinvest* time in whatever you'd like.

This stark realization also feeds back into Bill McDermott's urging to find (and live) that 25th hour each and every day since smart time utilization force-feeds goal attainment.

On average, each year people spend 267 hours *(11 days!)* waiting on something or someone. Invest those waits if possible. Turn downtime into *your* time.

As a quick example, whenever I travel on an airplane, I write. Plane time is *my* time. It used to be Wasted time, but now it's

214

Invested time. It's personal time, blocked to create. On crowded planes I sketch notes, concepts, ideas and double-check past strategic plans to see if I'm still on-course for completion. On less-crowded flights, I might spread out and write in rough draft or work on revisions.

Creating quality output to help others brings me a great sense of personal fulfillment. And if I'm not creating, I'm revisiting work and ideas I've already developed.

#6: **Zealously embrace the belief that using the "See the End" format enables you to say a lot despite writing very little.**

When developing these strategic plans, you won't have to write _much_ – but what you say and how you say it are vitally important.

In that regard, it's much like creating our Daily Dozen.

The Daily Dozen defines who we aspire to be in 12 succinct phrases. "See the End" strategic planning creates written road maps using minimal phrasing. It captures ideas and wastes no words in "netting them out."

Maximum effectiveness hinges on synthesizing, then succinctly crystallizing, your valuable strategic thoughts. The reason for the written simplicity is straightforward: If your plans are personal and need not be shared, there's no need for an essay; but if you present your "See the End" plan to others, you are consultatively sharing your vision. You are demonstrating a well-defined awareness of:

> a. *Where you are,*
>
> b. *Where you intend to end up,* and
>
> c. *How specifically you're going to get there.*

When presenting information, people speak between 120-and-180 words a minute. If that sounds like a lot, it's not. Most folks *think* at least four-to-five *times* that fast and read nearly that

215

quickly, too! Hence the compelling need for written brevity when presenting strategic plans to others.

So, our goal when presenting is to always to say a lot but *speak* a lot less. The degree of impact our plan will have depends largely on the words we select to convey a valuable message. A poorly thought out or weakly communicated message is why attentions wander during meetings and how *"Two-Puzzlers"* come into being.

There is a practiced art to organizing cogent thought and presenting it simply without a lot of rhetoric. The techniques we are about to work on are designed to teach you that skill.

After reviewing the "See the End" methods, you should emerge being able to do these four (4) things:

1. *Smartly organize and prioritize your thoughts.*

2. *Capture and succinctly describe the essence of those thoughts without excessive rhetoric.*

3. *Create plans that are rock-solid now – and yet malleable and able to change over time if necessary.*

4. *Produce a presentation format that's clean, simple, easy to understand and enables you to come across quite professionally when sharing your plan in group presentations.*

Your presentation will be a succinct, well-thought-out, organized and logical solution to what might otherwise seem to be a very difficult challenge.

#7: You must own of the "See The End" process and be consistent in Investing in its use.

If you trust this way of thinking and problem solving, *it will pay you back – big time!*

This approach allows you to soundly test the validity of your plan in both directions – from the end-vision backward to the

216

present state; and also from the current state *forward* – through your intermediate obstacles and directly to your end-vision.

When your plan makes sense in both directions (from the future looking back and the present to the future), it will be rock-solid and ready to execute with maximum effectiveness and minimal wasted time or effort.

After your plan is finished, polished and tested, the final result is your written road map. Follow it. Its flawless execution will deliver you to the unlocked door of your ambition.

Building *Your Own* Strategic Plans:
How to "See the End & Work Backward"

While at Xerox, I refined and utilized with great success a "top-down" pyramid approach that all starts with a well-defined end-vision or desired state. I named that goal my **Destination Objective.** My Destination is "the End" – the specific result I want to reach.

This format helped me greatly simplify and streamline my personal life, plus dramatically increase my effectiveness within the office. I used it to market hundreds of millions of dollars worth of complex business agreements.

Once you're stage four "Unconsciously Competent" and automatic using this technique, "See the End" will be a solution tool to help problem-solve anything in life – whether the challenge is large or small and exists inside the office or out.

As we begin learning to develop our plans, make sure to be sensitive to these three important things: *Building, Testing* and *Flawlessly Executing.*

On the following few pages are a step-by-step instructional method to learn precisely how to do this.

Building the Plan

Far and away the most important step is deciding what you want to have achieved once you are completely finished. That's your "end vision." If everything goes right and you pull off what you want to pull off, what exactly will have occurred?

Building the plan always starts here. You must first understand exactly what it is you want to be able to achieve.

Think through exactly what you want to achieve, then be prepared to describe it in just three (3) words.

Testing the Plan

Once your plan is in place, you'll want to test it – from your end-vision backward to the present. Testing the plan is critically important since it validates the soundness of what you're planning to do. It also serves to help identify loopholes to close.

If your plan stays sound as you moonwalk from your Destination Objective's end-vison all the way back to the present – then *great!*

Having survived the top-down test for strategic validity, turn around and test your plan from the bottom up – starting with the current state and validating each move you make progressing forward toward the top.

Simply put, the way you do that is simple. For each step in the plan, repeatedly ask yourself the same question: "If I do X and Y, will they result in Z occurring?" Every step should be tested and every step should validate "yes" as part of Testing.

The plan must make sense from both perspectives. If it doesn't, the plan's not correctly completed. It should be ironclad.

It's at this stage when you should also give your plan a good old-fashioned *"Reality Test."* Do you have the required *Knowledge*, *Skills* and *Attributes* to do what you want to do? If not, can you enlist the necessary resources to help? If so, is the use of those resources already factored into your strategy?

218

Soundly tested plans that pass the Reality Test can move mountains. Plans that won't pass the test never do.

Flawless Execution

Every step in your plan is assumed to be integral to the success of the strategy. And if every step *is* important, then it's critical to execute each action item as flawlessly as you can. The quicker you successfully complete every task and complete each step, the quicker your pyramid puzzle will be complete.

We *build* our plans from the top down – from the end vision backward to where we are today.

But we *complete* these challenges from the broad base of our current state *upward*.

When flawlessly executed, well-designed plans are thorough, precise and waste very little time or energy, since every objective is specific, necessary and crystal-clearly spelled-out.

Again, flawless execution underscores and reiterates the need to have already passed a Reality Check before you dive in headfirst. None of us can flawlessly execute even the greatest of plans if we don't have the KSA's to do so.

For easy reference and practice, in the back of the chapter I've included samples of a fully-completed plan, helpful reminder tips, and a blank pyramid practice sheet you can reproduce as needed.

There's also a chart with commonly used fill-in terms to help you quickly get the hang of the proper verbal format to use when developing your plans.

Thinking this way is a learned skill – and for most it requires just a little bit of practice. But once mastered, this strategic way of thinking becomes *how* you develop plans and problem-solve from this point forward.

This is a valuable, replicable *Life Skill* and I urge you to embrace it with confidence!

On the following page, we'll describe in specific detail and show, step by step, exactly how easy it is to complete.

(see charts beginning on next page)

Part 1:

"Identifying Your Destination."

&

Naming Your Action Plan

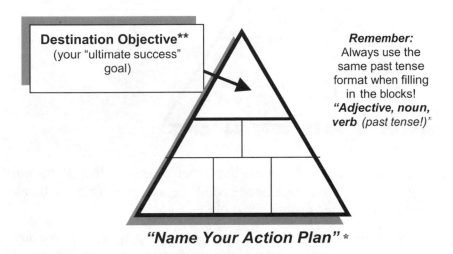

Destination Objective**
(your "ultimate success"
goal)

Remember:
Always use the
same past tense
format when filling
in the blocks!
*"Adjective, noun,
verb (past tense!)"*

"Name Your Action Plan" *

*1.) Label your Action Plan beneath the base of your pyramid. I recommend no more than a two or three-word name that clearly defines the challenge you're solving.

Don't get fancy – call it what it is.

"Career Management Strategy;" "Cost Reduction Initiative;" "Plan for Improved Fitness" are all examples. Label your pyramid clearly and simply.

2.) After you've named your pyramid, everything else shifts to identifying and properly naming the triangle's end-vision: Your ***Destination Objective.*

Always use the same fill-in format inside each pyramid block – adjective, noun, verb (all past tense). If our pyramid were named "Plan for Improved Fitness," our top end-goal would read something along the lines of *"Improved Fitness Achieved."*

221

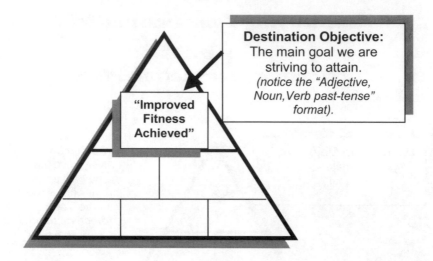

The ***Destination Objective*** is verbally defined inside the top "mini triangle" of the high peak end of the triangle. This top block succinctly describes *exactly* what our end-goal is.

By defining everything in our plan in <u>*past tense*</u>, we are assuming and demonstrating the expectation of its eventual achievement. This is very important during presentations to others. It conveys a strong message that you know what you want to do and know how to get there.

Judge for yourself. **Pick the statement that conveys a stronger message:** *"We've already done this,"* or **"We** *plan* **to do this."**

Which has a stronger impact on you as a listener?

The world has twice as many promises as it needs and half as many results. People want to hear about *results*. People want to *see* results. Psychologically, people are action-biased toward people who do things – who get things done. If you consistently convey the confident message that you *are* that type person, they will sign up to support a sound strategy.

It's from there – from the very top end-vision of our pyramid – that we'll build our strategic plan backwards.

222

Having filled in the top with *"Improved Fitness Achieved,"* next we'll work down though the center of the pyramid toward the broad base at the bottom. Our most important focus always remains on exactly where we're going and what must happen in order to get there.

3 Little Words

The **Destination Objective** *usually is described in just three (3) carefully selected words.* Remember that their order should always be the same: Adjective, noun, verb (all past tense). Rarely will you need more than three if you select the right ones.

A "cheat sheet" reference table of sample fill-in answers is in the back of this chapter. In it are adjectives, nouns and verbs you'll commonly use when creating your plans. All the words are listed in past tense so, as you work through several of these exercises, you can mix and match them while you get a feel for the flow and learn how to master this new method of strategic thinking. Remember:

a. The *ADJECTIVE* always goes first, and it is your description word. Words like "bigger, faster, longer, increased" and "decreased" are often used.

b. The *NOUN*, of course, is the subject of what your completion square's objective is centered around. Nouns are commonly people, places and things.

c. The *VERB* comes last and the very is the action word. In past tense, it serves to demonstrate the specific action you have taken and successfully completed.

As you learn the format, don't compromise the importance of proper word order. Make it a winning habit: *adjective-noun-verb (past tense).*

The more you use this technique, the more you'll appreciate continuity of completion. This will prove ultra-true during group presentations since the common format enables a smooth, cohesive professionalism throughout your entire delivery.

Part 2:

Positioning Yourself to Succeed . . . .
Selecting your Empowerment Objectives

Once we've got our end-goal defined and on-paper, our attention shifts to what has to be accomplished in order for our end-vision to result. If we plan and execute properly, the top of our pyramid should be the result of the two things beneath it being successfully completed.

Therefore, it's *critical* to study and select the *right* two things. We'll fill them in using the exact same *adjective-noun-verb (past tense)* format we've already embraced.

Our pyramid's middle row has two halves and they house your *Empowerment Objectives*. Your *Empowerments* are the two (2) things which *MUST HAPPEN* in order to produce your end-goal.

As you mull over what those two things might be, simply ask yourself this question: *"What two things simply must occur in order for me to reach my goal?"*

Keep it simple. Don't overcomplicate your plan. Zero rules exist that say strategic thinking must be overly complicated.

What strategic thinking *does* require is shrewd and smart clarity of thought.

Once you have a clearly-defined end vision in sight, *simply ask what two things must occur in order for that vision to become a reality.*

The answers to that simple question – those two challenges – are what goes in the middle row of your pyramid. *These are the two things that must be done successfully that empower you to succeed.*

Empowerment Objectives

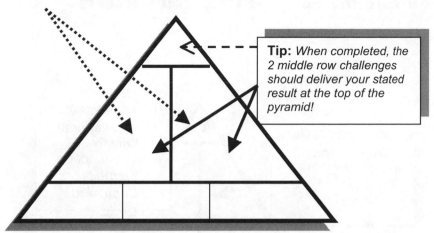

Tip: *When completed, the 2 middle row challenges should deliver your stated result at the top of the pyramid!*

Tip: At this point, remember to ask yourself this simple question:
"What two things MUST HAPPEN in order for me to reach my final goal?"

Once you've decided what those two things are, then test those two by asking this: *"If I achieve both these challenges, will they result in the attainment of my goal – my top-level Destination Objective?"*

The answer you are looking for must be an ironclad, absolute and airtight *"Yes!"*

If the answer is *"maybe," "probably," "not necessarily,"* or *"no,"* your two pivotal Empowerment Objectives need more fine-tuning.

If you think the challenge through carefully and deeply enough, nearly <u>every</u> Destination can be reached by completing just two mission critical puzzle pieces.

Some pieces simply take more turning and studying than others before they lock securely into place. But once you've got the critical two, congratulations – you've rounded the success corner and are headed for home.

Completion of your two Empowerment Objectives should *deliver* you to your Destination. Work hard to pick the right two.

How Empowerment Objectives
Fit into the Puzzle & Help You Succeed:

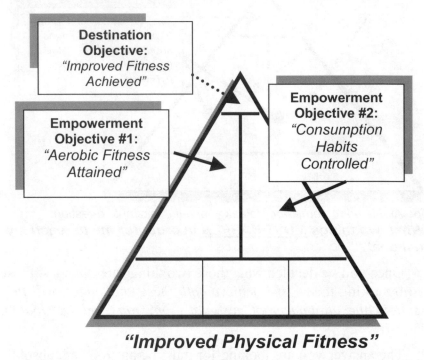

Destination Objective: *"Improved Fitness Achieved"*

Empowerment Objective #1: *"Aerobic Fitness Attained"*

Empowerment Objective #2: *"Consumption Habits Controlled"*

"Improved Physical Fitness"

It takes *both* of these Empowerment objectives to deliver improved fitness. Exercise alone won't do it without sensible eating and drinking habits. And dietary changes won't deliver fitness without the aerobic conditioning that must go with it.

These two things, combined together, *will* result in Improved Physical Fitness.

Part 3: *Plugging in Your Action Steps & Getting Started!*

Lastly, all that remains is to work backward from the *Empowerment Level* down toward the broad pyramid base by asking yourself the same basic question you did before. This baseline set of activities you'll identify are called **"Action Steps."**

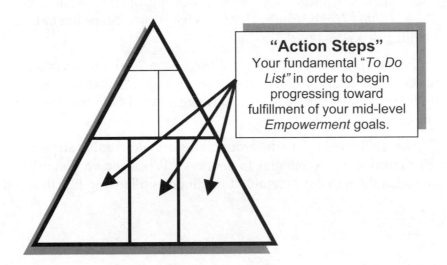

"Action Steps"
Your fundamental *"To Do List"* in order to begin progressing toward fulfillment of your mid-level *Empowerment* goals.

To determine the first of your **Action Steps**, take one of your mid-level challenges and ask yourself, *"What must I get done in order to make this occur? What are the interim things I need to complete in the short-term in order to position myself to be successful?"*

Let's continue using our "Improved Physical Fitness" pyramid as an example. Our two Empowerment Objectives were *"Aerobic Fitness Attained"* and *"Consumption Habits Controlled."* Let's study each one individually.

What thing (or couple of things) must occur before aerobic fitness can be attained? "Attained" means "reached and continued," so one workout by itself won't get us there. Clearly a cardiovascular exercise program must be created, practiced and regularly adhered to since fitness is earned over time, not overnight.

How do we capture those three thoughts in our *adjective-noun-verb (past tense)* format?

Our action steps might be "Medical clearance received," "Fitness program developed," and "Daily exercising maintained."

These Action Steps are good for one of our Empowerment goals – aerobic fitness – but what about the other? What about *"Consumption Habits Controlled?"* What Action Steps might lead to nailing down that one?

Perhaps "Dietary program followed" or "Caloric boundaries created," "Dietary limits respected," and "Evening snacks eliminated" are *all* things that contribute toward help manage our caloric intake.

Our challenge is to sift through all possible Action Steps and pick the critical few integral to success. When we've done that, and added them to our pyramid, it might end up looking like this:

(see chart on next page)

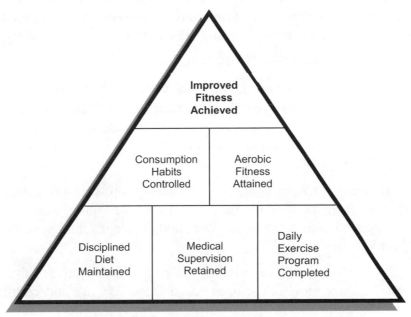

"Improved Physical Fitness"

Every appropriate mid-level Empowerment challenge must be Reality Tested and attainable. When they are, figuring out your Action Steps simply requires asking, *"What must get accomplished in order for that Empowerment challenge to become an achieved reality?"*

Your Action Steps must deliver you to the summit of *both* Empowerment challenges in order to reach the top of your selected mountain.

When they do – and when you have flawlessly executed your plan – you have earned the right to succeed. And you will.

Part 4: *Testing Your Plan*

Just as important as using every prudent possible resource to help build your plan is going through the process of testing it. Testing validates the airtight completeness of your strategy. Rather than assume it's correct – take the tougher view and assume

229

it isn't. Try and shoot holes in it. Better yet, hand it off to someone whose opinion you trust (and who hasn't seen it) and ask *them* to shoot holes in it. Encourage them to.

Testing is not difficult. But it *is* <u>necessary</u>.

1. Check that each block is completed using the past tense "*adjective, noun, verb*" format.

Simple examples of the proper format include: *"Lower Cost Achieved," "Faster Time-to-Market Delivered," "Dream Vacation Taken" and "New Beaver Dam Constructed."*

If you don't *have* continuity of completion, stop immediately and fix each box until they all read the same way – in demonstrated past tense with your thought clearly and succinctly captured.

I call the past-tense verbs at the end of each phrase "the *ed* words" – since most of the ones you'll frequently use end with the letters "*e*" and "*d.*"

2. Test the plan for top-down validity.

Test it from top-down by first asking if the description of your end-vision is 100% accurate and clear. If not, change it so it is.

Next, test your mid-row Empowerments by asking, "If I achieve these two Empowerment objectives, will my end-vision be the direct result?" If so, your two Empowerment objectives are *still* the keys to the kingdom.

If not, call a thought-provoking locksmith to help re-key them until they are. Resources have tremendous value during the planning stage, creation stage and especially the testing stage. Engage every necessary resource you can to accelerate your plan's achievement – but never think you won't benefit by engaging other pairs of eyes to help you through the darkest or most frustrating parts.

Lastly, test your Action Steps by having someone else answer the question concerning what must happen in order for your Empowerment Objective to be reached. The answer, hopefully, is identical to yours.

3. Re-test the plan for bottoms-up validity.

Next, validate the plan again. Only this time, go upward and start from the base. If you complete each Action Step in a quality way, will your desired Empowerment goals directly result? If not, chances are you missed a couple necessary Action Steps. Figure out what's missing, add them into the plan, then repeat the process. Test it again.

Once you've identified *exactly* what it takes to reach your Empowerment Objectives, simply ask that if you achieve both mid-level Empowerment challenges – *will your Destination Objective be the direct result?*

If you could complete your two mid-level Empowerment goals but not necessarily produce your hoped-for Destination, then there's a flaw at the Empowerment Level of the plan. You've got a gap you need to close. Get help, scrutinize it, and fix it. Adjust your Action Steps if necessary, also.

4. You may need more boxes or rows depending on the complexity of the challenge or the amount of detail you decide to delve into.

Remember: In effective strategic planning, everything starts at the finish line! Nail down that end-vision first, rock-solidly, and work backward from there.

Each plan will have only one Destination and, generally, you can reach that Destination with two carefully selected Empowerment achievements.

But in special cases you might need three. The answer to that key question ("How many?") always comes during the validation of the soundness of your plan: Whether it's two, three or even four Empowerments you must achieve, if you successfully complete them all, *will the result be the arrival at your Destination?*

The same holds true for your Action Steps. Don't get tripped up in minutiae. Keep things simple. Identify the critical few germane to success. Your plan might require only three significant action steps. Or you might identify four or five as mission-critical.

231

There is no absolute number you must have or "should" have. The quantity isn't important. What's important is that the ones you've identified are the ones you need to successfully position yourself to flawlessly execute your plan.

5. Flawless Execution – How to Do It.

The best plan in the world yields less than a crabapple tree unless you execute it properly. Be diligent and disciplined in staying the course.

a. **Never lose sight of the end.** Clearly *"See the End"* before plowing forward. Flawless execution demands never taking your eye off your end-vision.

b. **Pretend your plan is a submarine.** Make sure your sub is airtight before taking it out to sea. Reality Test your plan from the top down and then back up again.

Use all possible resources to built it, then all possible resources (preferably different ones) to help test it. Ask those resources to pull no punches. When it's a unanimous thumbs up, you're all set to pursue completion of your Action Steps.

c. **Always complete the plan the exact opposite of how you built it.** You *build* your plan from the top *down*. *Execute* the plan from the bottom *up*. Always execute your Action Steps first. Have persistent discipline and follow the map you've so carefully written, first steps first.

d. **Shortcuts can do more harm than good.** The bigger the stakes, the more essential it is not to cave in to the lure of shortcuts. Smart poker players play the face cards they hold, not the ones still buried in the deck.

e. **Timing: The Two-headed Coin of Reality.** Like it or not, timing has a lot to do with success. Keep that in mind as you craft your plans and outline the necessary steps you have to take.

232

The timing of *some* things is controllable. Others aren't. If your plan is written around a lot of things beyond your control, then don't expect an easy road to success.

Plans that are susceptible to potential timing problems might require Plan B. Plan B is an alternative solution – a different way to capture the flag. Strategic plans often involve re-crafting alternative methods. No need to panic: Simply draw up another plan. See the *new* end and work backward from there.

Expect bad timing to cause you to step sideways or backward. Executing an important plan sometimes is like dancing a waltz: Two steps forward and one to the side. Hopefully the timing disruptions are merely temporary inconveniences and won't cause you to have to sit out the entire dance.

Smart planners anticipate and factor into the equation possible delays where developing their strategy. If the situation warrants, proactively plan on what portion of the plan might be slowed down and prepare alternative solutions that might get you quickly back on track.

The bigger the plan, the more thorough and well-tested it needs to be for soundness.

Airtight plans are nearly always executable.

"See the End & Work Backward"
Order-of-Completion Guide

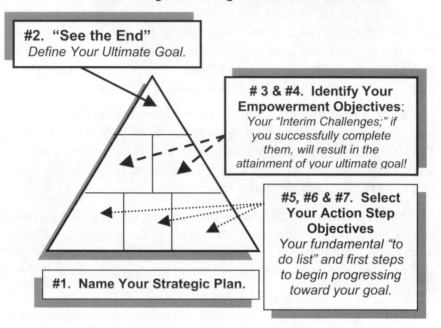

#2. "See the End"
Define Your Ultimate Goal.

 # 3 & #4. Identify Your Empowerment Objectives: *Your "Interim Challenges;" if you successfully complete them, will result in the attainment of your ultimate goal!*

#5, #6 & #7. Select Your Action Step Objectives *Your fundamental "to do list" and first steps to begin progressing toward your goal.*

#1. Name Your Strategic Plan.

1. *Name your strategic plan.*

Don't get fancy: Be clear, concise and call it what it is. Three or four well-chosen words should be plenty.

2. *"See the End" – and accurately define it.*

This is your *Destination Objective.* When everything's completed, this is exactly what you want to have occurred.

3. *& 4: Decide on the two (2) precise mid-level Empowerment Objectives that enable you to be successful.*

When you've successfully completed both, the direct result and what they produce should be your Destination Objective. In other words, ask yourself: *"If I successfully complete X + Y, will Z be the direct result?"*

5, 6, & 7: *Identify your necessary Action Steps.*

Your *Action Steps* get you going. Laundry-list a bunch, then select the necessary few. Don't get bogged down in non-essentials.

Your list of Action Steps might be long or short, depending on what you're trying to do and how new the challenges are.

The beauty in mastering this "See the End" format is its sheer simplicity and broad-range versatility. This is a valuable life skill. You can use it to achieve important goals in your daily life, and also during the organization of business strategies.

It's the quickest and best way I've ever found to cut through the clutter and draw a straight line from where I am to where I want to be.

On the next couple pages are valuable sample sheets to help you practice the "See the End" technique.

Practice it, master it, trust it and use it. Strive to become unconsciously competent with the technique. Once learned, it will never let you down. And it won't let down anyone you teach it to, either.

Good luck. Learn, and have fun with the format. Once you build it right, your plan will work like a good Swiss watch!

"See the End & Work Backward"
Pyramid Completion Cheat Sheet

Mix-and-Match from each column and get in the word-order habit of using first Column A, then B, then C. The more you practice, the quicker you'll become unconsciously competent at thinking this way. Proper word choice is important. Always select the best possible words to clearly describe your message.

A Personal & Business *Adjectives*	B Common *Nouns* for Various Challenges	C Common and Helpful *Verbs (past tense)*
Improved	Fitness	Achieved
Superior	Performance	Demonstrated
Physical	Well-being	Improved
Bad	Habits	Halted
Fiscal	Responsibility	Delivered
Foremost	Challenge	Completed
Personal	Ambition	Finished
Lifelong	Dream	Attained
Critical	Skills	Sharpened
Negative	Behaviors	Terminated
Hurtful	Relationships	Ended
Wasted	Money	Stopped
Retirement	Savings	Started
Old	Friends	Retained
New	Hobby	Initiated
Important	Talent	Mastered
Competitive	Accounts	Penetrated
Existing	Departments	Researched
Critical	Strategies	Decided
Initial	Findings	Validated
Prudent	Recommendation	Proposed
Older	Products	Replaced
Quality	Installation	Begun
Annual	Goals	Overachieved
Potential	Clients	Surveyed
Conventional	Thinking	Challenged
Discretionary	Funding	Approved
Performance	Barriers	Hurdled
Unnecessary	Risks	Measured

REMEMBER:

Destination **(top):** Your ultimate goal.

Empowerments **(mid-row):** What you must accomplish for your ultimate achievement to occur.

Action Steps **(base):** The initial activities you must complete in order to reach your Empowerments and position yourself to be successful.

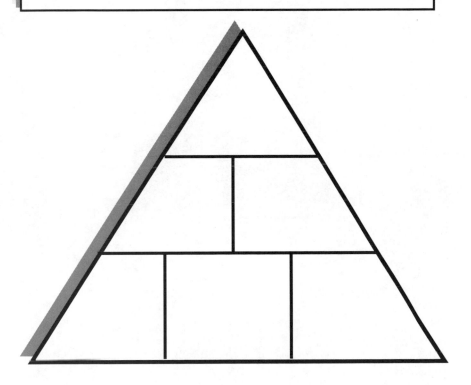

(Name Your Strategic Plan)

Chapter 13

LIFE IS A 4-LETTER WORD

"Life" is the most perfectly spelled word in the language. Four letters, each in perfect order and standing for something important: "**L**ife **I**s **F**requently **E**motional."

Life *is* emotional. It's *supposed* to be. When it isn't, then maybe we aren't living it right. Mortality, my friends, is often inconvenient.

Noted behaviorist Morris Massey slots the formulation of our life values into four life-stage categories. During these four-stages of personality formation, five primary influences shape our lives: Our family (both immediate and intergenerational), our friends, our religion, the schooling we receive and our surrounding geography.

From birth through the age of 7, we imprint from our parents or guardians.

From 8-to-13 we model behaviors from others, often other family members and people in our immediate contact and friendship circle. Midway through this stage – by the age of 10 – Massey says a full <u>90%</u> of our values systems are already firmly locked into place.

Then, from age 14-through-19, our behaviors are shaped and influenced by socialization – by peers, for example. I think labeling it the "socialization period" is Massey's nice way of calling them "The Horrible Teen Years."

By the age of 20, our values and personalities are pretty much locked-in.

Beyond that, only one thing will change us: The emotional earthquakes and aftershocks of Significant Emotional Events.

Each of our lives is shaped and re-shaped by the random series of major emotional influences we experience. These life-shaping instances change us – hopefully for the better, but sometimes for the worse.

Whenever you've weathered one, one thing's for sure – you are *not* the same person you were before it occurred. Like it or not – ready or not – you change. Your views change, your attitudes change and your values change.

For a quick example, remember what J.K. Rowling said: She would not have written Harry Potter's character the way she did had she not suffered through the loss of her mother.

The death permanently changed Rowling and those very same changes were directly reflected in how she thought. J. K. expressed herself on paper and her attitudes flowed from her mind, through her fingers and directly into her characters.

There are two types of Significant Emotional Events we typically deal with – the *Controllable* and the *Uncontrollable*.

Controllables are self-created. Uncontrollables are thrust upon us by forces we can't do anything about. We are the recipients, not the creators.

No two sets of life experiences are the same, so no two sets of Significant Emotional Events are, either. Let's take a look at the chart on the next page for some common catalysts that change our lives.

Look at the list on the left of the page and carefully think about the things that have suddenly re-shaped your life to this particular point in time. Chances are pretty good they'll fall into one of the eight categories.

Common Significant Emotional Events

	Occurrence (*what happened, to whom?*)	Expected or Unexpected?	Was It Preventable or Totally Uncontrollable?	Were You *Directly* or *Indirectly* Affected?
1	*Tragic Loss* (*relatives, friends, co-workers*)			
2	*Near Misses & Close Calls*			
3	*Illnesses & Scares* (*including alcohol & drugs*)			
4	*Love & Romance* (*winning & losing*)			
5	*Brushes with Fame* (*both positive & negative*)			
6	*Judgment Errors* (*personal & professional*)			
7	*Job-related* (*fair & unfair*)			
8	*Pure Luck* (*good & bad*)			

As you examine the list of eight common causes (above), think through your own life experiences and select the one experience in each category that's affected your life the most.

Each identified event has helped shaped who you are today and chances are they strongly influenced the Daily Dozen list you crafted for yourself earlier on.

Think, too, about *how old you were* when each one occurred. Experiencing a Significant Emotional Event is like being tattooed. Even early in life, the darn thing sticks with you – deeply and forever.

The Eight (8) Common Causes
of
Significant Emotional Events ("SEE's")

1. *Tragic Loss*

There is a natural order in life. The inescapable truth is that in every family, one survivor will bury all the others. A disruption in that natural order is more difficult to deal with that the eventual death of a loved one who's lived a good, long life.

I lost one parent expectedly (cancer) and the other unexpectedly (heart attack). Neither was preventable but two packs of cigarettes a day might lend a healthy argument that each death was premature. I was directly affected by both losses but understood the natural order of mortality. My father even spoke of it at my mother's graveside, quietly saying to all four children that one of us in the family would bury the other five.

A decade or so ago a close friend I hadn't seen in way too long finally coordinated schedules and teed it up for a private round of golf. We caught up on everything: Work, wives, kids, problems, you name it – we covered it. When we finished, we hugged goodbye.

Twelve hours later, he was dead in a plane crash. I was devastated.

Another tragedy happened just a couple years ago. I was working in Hawaii and a co-worker snapped, shooting and killing seven other co-workers. The police ordered us to leave the office

242

and disperse throughout Honolulu. I was about 300 yards away when the police apprehended the killer that afternoon in a nearby park.

A month before this book was published, the fellow who was supposed to read the final manuscript was killed in the terrorist attack on New York and the Pentagon.

There for the grace of God go any of us. Each of these events profoundly impacted my life and changed the way I now live it.

2. *Near Misses & Close Calls*

Who *hasn't* had a near-fatal car crash or mid-air emergency? What about crimes committed against you or your family? There's an old saying that close calls sometimes help people "find religion." A brush with death certainly *can* shape how we live our lives from that point forward. Many people prefer to know their maker on a first-name basis *before* the day suddenly arrives that they're unexpectedly introduced.

3. *Illnesses & Scares*

One of my closest friends recently was told to get his affairs in order after a lump was removed from his throat. A week later, tests came back – against all odds – that the tumor was benign, not malignant after all. An avid golfer, he doesn't much worry about 3-putt greens any more.

Scares and illnesses often give us a second chance to reshape our lives. Ideally, we should all hope to be a little more proactive and not wait until these types of traumas are experienced first-hand in order to re-craft our values.

4. *Love & Romance*

Some shapings are due to physical things. Others are purely emotional. The head, the heart and the soul carry three separate briefcases. Many are the men and women who've opened their hearts to love only to be rejected. For many, the hurt of rejection causes permanent scarring and a future reluctance to ever risk putting so much emotional vulnerability in destiny's outstretched hands held by anyone else.

Great love is like great success. Both require a great amount of risk.

But love and romance can have wonderfully positive Significant Emotional Event impact, also. I never really knew how to love *anything* until I joined the ranks of surprised husbands who became a somewhat reluctant father. A dozen years later, I can't imagine a life without her mother – or her.

5. Brushes with Fame

We are such a celebrity-crazed society, it's startling how much influence well-known people can have on the lives of others. Personal interactions with high profile personalities can change lives for better or worse.

People with a passion in life will follow leaders demonstrating excellence in pursuit of the very same passion.

Negative acts (hate crimes, for example) can also trigger the ushering of an impressionable individual to either the right or wrong fork in the behavioral road of his or her life.

6. Mistakes in Judgment

Who among us hasn't made a bushel basket of these? Some, certainly, reshape who we are and how we live our future. Learn to own the mistakes you make. This is especially true in the business world. There is unlimited power in the truth. Outgrow the mistakes you make by taking their lessons, embracing them, and moving on.

7. Job-related: Fair & Unfair

My father was let go from his job at the age of 53. He never got over it and was very unhappy throughout the last 10 years of his life.

Changes in business climate necessitated those cutbacks at a corporate level and as a line manager, there wasn't much – if anything – he could do to avoid or control his job-related destiny.

For your own emotional safety, always remember to live a life that defines yourself way beyond just what you do for a living. *Work is what you do to pay the bills.* Leave its boundaries there whenever you can.

If you're rich without money, you'll weather the emotional trauma of a job loss far better than my dad. In the long run, you'll be fine. The bigger your goodness portfolio, the easier you'll handle a surprise.

8. Pure Luck: Good & Bad.

There's something to be said for pure, dumb, falling-from-the-sky good fortune. People win lotteries. Or so I hear. But people also build and lose their dream house and life's possessions due to a freak fire, mudslide, or (in some countries) a military takeover. Luck – both good *and* bad – reshapes lives every single day.

Extreme luck – either kind – is uncontrollable so treat it accordingly. If it's good – be grateful and stay true to your core values.

If it's bad – then manage by fact and only worry about what you *can* control. Develop plans to move forward and force your temporarily dispirited self to take action steps that help move yourself forward. When you do that – when you take those steps forward – the view changes. And when the view changes, so does your perspective.

The above list contains eight major categories that produce most of life's most Significant Emotional Events. Regardless of the source of the life-shaping influence, it's vitally important to keep these three points concerning SEE's in the forefront of your mind:

a) SEE's are normal and inevitable. Significant Emotional

Events are as much a part of daily life as sunrises and sunsets. They are the earthquakes between those sunsets. The tremors and aftershocks are unbiased. They shake the shoes of everyone.

Expect them. They will come. And they will go.

Regardless of whether you decide to go out and give of yourself to consciously create positive SEEs for others, or simply lay on your sofa while life spins by, sooner or later, the tremors will rumble through your reality. You, and those around you, will be affected. Count on it.

b) They are either controllable, or, uncontrollable. As we learned back in Chapter 3 when we talked about The Worry Circle, the only things in life worth worrying about are those things *we* have direct control over.

If you, or someone you know, is dragging around the wreckage of a Significant Emotional Event that stems from something *beyond* anyone's direct control, then the focus should immediately shift from dwelling on it to figuring out how to emerge with a positive learning experience.

And if the situation *is* controllable, we learned in Chapter 12 how to develop a quick, smart, action plan to help fuel positive change. In those cases, sit down and draw up a smart plan to make things better. See the End – where you or a friend would like to emerge – and work backward to where you are. Then take the first flawlessly-executed step forward.

We all own a compelling need to help others "let go of the past." The past is uncontrollable and unchangeable and weathering a SEE is like battening-down during an emotional hurricane. Hurricane winds blow terribly until the eye of the storm arrives – then it briefly gets calm again. The eye is still. But the weather changes as the storm moves on.

Expect the winds of tragedy to resume blowing as soon as the eye passes by. Put trust and faith in knowing that the further away the eye travels, then slower blow the winds. Soon enough that particular storm will be gone, for good, the sun will shine and the birds will be chirping in the trees. The vibrant colors of living will once again surround you.

The fastest way to let go of the past is to better the future of others. Take it to heart, and coach and counsel others to feel that way, too.

c) ***Remember that SEE's are rarely reversible.*** Consider Significant Emotional Events to be life's medicine chest. Some medicines taste pretty good; others taste miserably bitter. All of them, regardless of how they taste, are designed to help you weather the illnesses that come with living a long, healthy well-balanced life.

Don't fight it: Take your medicine, swallow hard, blink twice, and look forward to tomorrow. It will be a better day. By doing so, you are courageously shaping yourself into being a better person.

Always reach out to help others, too. People generally internalize when hit with emotional trauma. Being alone with a head jammed full of despair and emotionally stormy seas sloshing back and forth between the ears can make the stoutest of sailors seasick and miserable.

Don't wait for people you care about to find their own way back into port. Go get them and tow them back in.

Summary

After the age of 20, defining moments, both good and bad, continually shape and re-shape our adult lives. Frequently these moments come attached to quite a bit of emotion – either positive or negative. Sorrowful emotional events, frustratingly, seem to outweigh the joyful ones – if you let them.

Sorrowful events *will* happen. If they don't – you don't care enough *about* enough. Few are those immune to unpredictable pain.

The very nature of mortality's realities programs Significant Emotional Events into life's remote control and Reality punches that darn *PLAY* button from time-to-time just to force us to sit through and pay rapt attention to a Reality show we'd rather not be bullied into seeing.

Happy, joyful Significant Emotional Events can be built – if you care enough to make them. Helping shape a positive defining life moment for someone else is one of living's purest rewards. The memory stays with you both forever. And as you go through life and look back on enriching the life of someone else, the feeling of goodness will still be standing there – tall and proud like a lighthouse beacon beaming powerfully through a moonless night.

These Significant Emotional Events will arrive unannounced, cloaked in many different uniforms. How you react to, then handle, their associated emotional traumas – both good and bad – mightily shapes your future. They also influence important decisions you need to make as you arrive at forks in the road before you.

Regardless, when it comes to living, one thing remains steadfast and absolute: The inevitable inevitably happens.

With the inevitable comes the correlated truism that all of us – at one point or another – take turns in the barrel. Each of us will have to weather our very own set of uncontrollable Significant Emotional Events.

To use a baseball example, a fastball is easier to hit for most hitters than a curveball. The reason is that a fastball comes in straight. If you time your swing right, you'll probably hit it even if it's really fast.

Curves are harder to hit. They swoop in with a bending arc and you can't swing where the ball is, but instead where it will be. You have to guess and react to its changes in-flight.

Much of life is batting practice and hittable fastballs. But occasionally Fate decides to throw a wicked, hardbreaking curve. We swing and miss. Or someone around us does. The curveball's surrounding trauma of illnesses and death reshape not only own lives but the lives of people around us. How *we* handle those setbacks can influence others, too.

When diagnosed with a terminal case of A.L.S., Hall of Fame baseball pitcher Jim "Catfish" Hunter took one of the worst conceivable hands anyone could be dealt and turned it into a dignified positive by helping raise research money and awareness so others behind him might escape a similar fate.

To some extent, we're all links in a chain. How Hunter handled *his* Significant Emotional Event directly influenced others on the periphery of his illness and how *they* reacted to, too. Jimmy's courage made positive change happen for many lives – including countless strangers.

Life changes over time and Significant Emotional Events will subtly sneak up on you – sometimes in disguise. For example, I remember *exactly* where I was when someone called me "sir" for the first time (and meant it). Fishing off an ocean pier in Jacksonville, Florida, a scruffy teenager not much younger than I walked toward me and addressed me that way.

At that precise moment I realized that in the eyes of the rest of the world I wasn't a kid any longer. I was now a sir. Suddenly I'd finished doing what I set out to do four years before when I left home to go to college: I had crossed the river from cocky teenager to fledgling adult.

I leaned on the pier's southside railing and stared south down the beach toward St. Augustine. "This," I finally decided, "Is a *good* thing. A scary thing, but a good thing."

With that moment came the ownership to act like an adult. My entire outlook on life changed. One simple phrase from a teenager needing a shave snapped me into a different perspective like smelling salts under the nose of a groggy prizefighter.

Life flies by and mirrors, unfortunately, aren't like photographs. Mirror images perpetually change, adding lines and creases when bad things happen and smiles and dimples when good things do.

Every chugging rollercoaster pauses at the top, then hurtles back down. While life sometimes seems less a ride and more like a pro wrestling match against a bad guy of evil and devious means, always remember that if you live true to your Daily Dozen – in the end – the bad guy will get his just reward and *you* will emerge victorious.

You simply have to stay the course. Life *is* frequently emotional. It's *supposed* to be. Expect some rough weather from time to time but remember the sun will shine again.

Love the life you've been given and, for better or worse, do your best to love the scenic ups and bewildering downs of the journey it takes you on, too.

Chapter 14

Closing the Studio Door

8 Short Hops to Life on the Pro Leisure Tour

Several years ago I was working in Seattle and went to Jazz Alley to hear famed jazz pianist McCoy Tyner. I'd heard of Tyner but never seen him play. It was a mid-week after-dinner show and the club was only one-third full.

Since my hearing isn't good on my right side, I asked to be seated somewhere my left ear could face the small stage. The hostess took me right down front, to a small table five feet from where Tyner would sit and play.

Tyner, to a crowded room of empty chairs, played to a level of greatness I'd never heard before. Much of the time his eyes were closed. He played with his heart – his fingers simply delivered the message. When the show ended, I thanked him for giving those few of us who came that night a very special evening to remember.

As I drove back down First Avenue past Pike Place Market and toward the Alexis Hotel, I replayed in my mind the greatness of what I'd seen and heard. I wondered what it felt like for a brilliant musician like McCoy Tyner to close the recording studio door and walk out alone, into the night, after creating what he surely must know is a magical piece of music.

The world's airwaves are filled with hits – all written and recorded by an individual or group of individuals – and all dependent upon a vast network of supporting players to deliver that music around the world for others to enjoy.

Music is a team industry, certainly, but for the creator of the music and writer of the lyrics, there's an intimate, solitary personal moment – however long or brief it might be – that's reserved for the quiet time following creation where they pause to reflect on what they've just achieved.

That intimate time of reflection causes a warm personal glow of satisfaction that radiates from within. It envelops every good emotion that makes life worth living.

We *all* have these moments. We *all* create great music. Our music in life simply takes different forms. Our mission is to create as much of that music as we possibly can – to feel that warm, satisfying personal glow every chance possible.

Those feelings – those emotions – are what Living Life on the Pro Leisure Tour is all about. We all have PLT moments – but better yet is living an entire PLT lifestyle.

To safely cross the river from where we are today to life on the PLT simply requires mixing four easy steps with eight short hops as you make your way across the series of stream-strewn rocks that rise dryly above the water's surface. By taking one measured move – then the next – we'll soon reach the far bank and life on the PLT.

Every chapter you've read so far is one or the other: A quick easy step or a flat rock to hop onto. The four steps are easy. We can safely reach each with a single stride.

Each rock to hop onto, however, is a different size – as are challenges. They're also different distances from each other – just like goals. The eight short hops take us from rock-to-rock and all the way across the river. Some hops require a little more airborne bravado than others.

The river isn't deep and no one drowns attempting to cross. Some of us might slip from time-to-time. That's to be expected – the underwater sides of river rocks often grow slippery moss. So, working our way completely across the river involves not only careful attention to the nature of each rock we're hopping onto, but also a conscious awareness of where the slippery moss might be.

Step by step and hop by hop, let's take a chapter-reviewing look at the route we've traveled to get from where we were in The Past to where we want to be in The Future.

Easy Step "A": *Venturing across the Bridge to Reality*

The Bridge to Reality traversed our lovable teen years and led us across the post-high school valley to Adulthood. Whether we went to college or didn't, once we arrived at Adulthood we all soon realized that much of what we needed to learn about life wasn't taught in school.

What we *really* needed to learn would continue to be force-fed over time – whether we liked it or not and whether the lessons seemed fair or not.

This was an easy step to make since so many people were crowded behind us, shoulder to shoulder, bumping and pushing us forward. Ready or not, we had to keep shuffling across that bridge.

Easy Step "B": *Deciding to be Rich Without Money*

As we traveled around and saw more of the country and more of the world, we soon realized that we have a much better life than so many millions in our country and billions more scattered throughout all corners of the globe. We learned the importance of being more grateful for what we have and less worried about what we don't.

We learned to strive for a life that's Rich Without Money – a cognizant state of awareness that helps motivate us to step off the comfort of the shore and begin to ford the river before us.

Like walking across the Bridge to Reality, appreciating our life's baseline is not a difficult step. Everyone should be able to take it. With so much to be grateful for already, why not maximize the opportunity we've all been given?

Hop #1: *Deciding it's important to live life with a positive and contented Pro Leisure Tour attitude.*

The courage to hop to a rock comes from seeking a destination worth the risk. And Life on the PLT is worth getting wet to reach.

Living Life on the Pro Leisure Tour means embracing its attitudes, values and achievements. It requires a zest and urgency for living. Above all, the toll for admission involves developing a sense of contentment with the Who, What, When, Where, Why and How of your own personal being.

Who do you truly aspire to be? What will you choose to worry about? When are you smart to switch jobs? Where will you most likely expect to find roadbocks to your goals – and how will you go about getting rid of them? Why should you live your life with a sense of urgency? And when you want to achieve something important, how will you set about creating a smart strategic plan you can execute flawlessly?

All of these things – the "5-W's *("who, what when, where, why")* and the How" – are important components of life on the PLT. Prior to methodically achieving each one, your first Short Hop to the closest big rock in front of you requires the conscious decision that it's a hop worth taking. If life on the PLT is where you want to end up, then flex your knees, make like a frog, inhale deeply and go *"boing!"*

Moss Alert: As with every rock you'll hop toward, slippery moss rings and clings to its underwater side. The moss for pursuing a Life on the PLT is living a live that's *out* of balance instead of *in* it. You can't hope to land and keep your balance if you're out of balance when you jump.

The moss will also splash us if we don't keep the endorphins flowing or let the Worry Circle manage *us* instead of vice-versa.

Hop #2: *Signing up to own our Daily Dozen.*

Every explorer needs to know their inner self before setting out on an important trip. You have to know who you are, what you aspire to be, and sign up to strive to become what you say. It takes courage to script the fiber of your being. It takes even *more* courage to live it.

Hopping atop the Daily Dozen rock takes valor and a fearless spirit. It's hard to consciously decide to challenge yourself to be better tomorrow than you are today. The jump to the Daily Dozen rock requires a deep-knee bend and determined push-off. It's a leap-frog hop that quizzes your fortitude.

Moss Alert: Halfhearted hops will come up short. If you say it – but don't live it – you'll get wet. You'll land in the river. Chances are you'll flop and fall backward and splashily land on the big round muscles of your keister.

But, you'll *never* slip on moss when you live your values.

A lot of adults abandon their dreams as they age. They shouldn't. But the reason they do is that they can't see the road to reach them. That road starts with deciding the dream is worth pursuing, then following that decision by shaping yourself into a deserving person able to *earn* that dream's fulfillment. There is a price that must be paid – a personal improvement price – in order to proceed.

Pay that price and you'll stand on high, dry ground. You've earned the right to keep advancing.

Easy Step "C": *Respecting the falling sand inside the Hourglass of Time.*

The next stone in the river is an easy one. The large flat rock is invitingly close so no leaping is required.

We all have a limited, finite and ever-dwindling number of Personal Days to achieve the non-business-related things in life that mean the most to us. Our Personal Days are skewed toward our youth and old age. In-between, during our working careers, we must treasure, protect and *invest* those precious days to help us stay in life balance. Every single one is too valuable to waste.

By the very nature of its round-the-clock demands, maternal responsibilities refuse to allow the daily separation of responsibilities. For women, the sanctity of protecting these vitally important Personal Days is extra-important.

Personal Days give us the chance to rest, re-charge our batteries and have fun. Whenever we're ready, we'll size up the next rock in the river and get ready to leap for it.

Hop #3: *Knowing when to switch jobs – and* <u>WHY</u>.

Work's what we do to pay the bills. So, if the money's rolling in and paying the bills, financial pressure shouldn't be a concern. But we also know that our work *attitude* plays a huge factor in the quality of life we feel we're living.

We can either cherish, invest, spend or waste our time at work. Those hours quickly add up and heavily and directly impact how we feel about the overall life we're living.   When it comes time to change jobs, we want to run *toward* something we've got a passion for – or hope to grow a passion for over time.

Moss Alert: If we're unhappy at work and quit to run *from* something, chances are we'll land off-balance at our next job, slip on the moss and fall in the river. Repositioning your professional life to take on a new career challenge isn't always convenient – in fact it rarely is – but it's always worthwhile if you're running toward something you'd really love to do.

Hop #4: *Deciding to be a Thriver.*

Whatever you choose to do in life – be good at it. *Thrivers* are maximum achievers with high-performance traits worth admiring and emulating. Thrivers are made, not born, so our challenge is two-fold: Aspiring to be one; then becoming one.

Survivors are usually minimalists – the left-end of the performance bell curve. Don't be one. For some, it's a temporary stage en route to a better life. Help them.

Drivers are the workforce majority. From the Drivers grow the Thrivers. But it's at the apex of the bell curve – its middle – where performers are average. And being average means we're just as close to the bottom as we are to the top.

Thrivers aspire to be, and stay, to the far right of the bell curve. They find no joy in being average if their KSA's hold the potential for more.

Moss Alert: If you can't accurately self-assess where you truly belong, you'll slip off the rock. The real and introspective truth often delivers a line in the sand that marks the true beginning of your new journey forward.

Your self-assessment should be identical to what your boss and associates would say. If you rely solely on your own point-of-view, you are more likely to overestimate than underestimate your talents. Doing so is normal – it's human nature.

For example, a recent survey revealed that 80% of people in America consider themselves to be among the top 20% best looking. While beauty is subjective and certainly in the eye of the beholder, there's a big, big gap between those two numbers.

Narrow your self-assessment reality gap and you'll narrow the chance of slipping off the rock.

Hop #5: *Realizing success is no accident and that KSA's & Success Probability are as intertwined as hair braids and wool sweaters.*

Success requires the weaving a tapestry of sufficient Knowledge and Skills with winning Attributes. Every challenge requires a certain level of each in order to successfully attain its completion. Maximum success requires the disciplined blending of all three.

The accumulation of relevant *Knowledge* seems like a bottomless pit but every kernel you toss in increases our potential proficiency.

Skills are learned, not ordained, and require continuous improvement. They require practice, repetition, coaching and counseling.

Attributes are the unique set of performance tangibles each of us possess. They measure they "want to" that motivates each one of us to succeed to the level we want to achieve – be that Thriver, Driver, or just a Survivor. Pride and ego often drive a top performer. To them, winning matters.

The toughest of the three KSA's to judge are the Attributes since they're more subjective than objective.

Moss Alert: Not knowing *what* you need to know will cause you to slip. So will getting lazy and not continuously honing the skills you've got while simultaneously developing new ones. And you can pretty much guarantee you'll get wet if you put forth a half-baked effort rather than your best.

There's a performance discipline involved with showcasing a winner's Attributes. If you compromise applying your Knowledge and Skills with anything less than a winner's determination, you better wear a swimsuit.

Hop #6: *Determinedly Detouring around Roadblocks to Performance.*

Once we set out to achieve something and find ourselves temporarily derailed, the cause is one of three things: Either the problem's a *Can't do it, Won't do it,* or *Prevented From doing it*.

Some challenges we simply do not have the skills to achieve. Others we *can* accomplish if given more instruction or training.

A *Won't do it* usually stems from a lack of incentive. The incentives can be either positive (a reward, bonus, etc.) or negative. Negative incentives are usually punitive.

Adding a reward (good or bad) to solve a *Won't do it* performance problem should be instilled only in the spirit of eliminating the behavior once and for all.

Moss Alert: Performance problems should be proactively analyzed, action-planned and resolved. Every moment you dawdle or waste prior to dissecting what's gone wrong is gone for good. Time is far more valuable than money. Why waste it by being reactive instead of proactive?

If you've got a problem and you can't figure out why, you'll wobble off the rock and fall in unless you reach out for help. Seek assistance. Get someone to steady you atop the rock. If something's not going right but you're not sure why, proactively turn to a trusted resource and seek a new perspective.

Volunteer to help others around you too. Both in the home and in the office, be proactive helping others keep their balance on the performance rock. After all, you're already two-thirds of the way across the river – no sense falling in now.

Easy Step "D": *Avoid being sealed inside "The Octagon of Mediocrity."*

The Octagon sports eight invisible walls designed to trap us inside a less-than-Thriving level of daily performance. We can outgrow these walls, scale them for good and leave them permanently behind.

We vow to avoid stepping on the Hamster Wheel to Nowhere unless forced to. We have no interest in being average – we want and expect to succeed – and respect the sublime fairness of having to earning the right to succeed or fail at whatever we pursue. We understand the difference between being given a chance and earning the right to try.

We know ourselves very well – our strengths *and* limitations – and have decided to be an impact player – not a role player – at home, in the community or in the office. Hopefully we aspire to be an impact player in everything we do.

We realize that technology provides tools that enable us to do more and that technology's offspring are not inanimate objects to hide behind at the expense of physical exercise or social interaction. Their role is simply to enable us to do get more done, quickly.

We take a pride in not being know-it-alls but rather being someone fascinated with the chance to make important learning discoveries every single day. We realize that the more we know, the less we don't.

Lastly, we are very well aware that we are whom we hang out with. If we aspire to achieve more, we need to hang out with more achievers. If we aspire to learn more, we must gravitate toward activities where that will happen.

We remain forever secure in knowing that we'd rather be a bright light on a Broadway marquee than an unused flashlight in the glove compartment of an old parked car.

The Octagon of Mediocrity is the Alamo of the Average. It's much easier and much more tempting to do nothing at all than it is to determinedly try to achieve something new and difficult. It's easier to stay trapped inside than tunnel underneath.

Leaving the comfort zone of the Octagon's confines takes a bit of determination and spirit not everyone has. If you are scared to seek new ideas, experience new things, learn about new topics and differing points of view, well, then you are probably too timid to venture beyond the walls. And in those cases, you'll be very hard-pressed to maximize your true potential.

Avoid the risk of being trapped like a mime inside the invisible box. Outgrow the Octagon and remain resolute that your view of it will be from the outside looking in, as opposed to being stuck inside, looking out.

Easy Step "E": *Realizing that unfailing passion, hard work, and acting with a sense of urgency*

will leave footprints on the proud sandy beach of personal achievement.

There's no substitute for faith in your own ability and confidence that what's important to you is also important to others.

There will be defining times in your life you have to have courage. Courage to persevere and follow your dreams, and courage to realize that living with a true sense of urgency will enrich your life in a thousand positively spoking directions. It's a lot easier to lay on a sofa and do nothing than proactively seek and take on new challenges that break old habits, challenge your skills and fuel a newly-kindled personal passion.

These ideals require embracing. You've got to grab on and squeeze them tight. You've got to make them yours.

Great achievements require a bit of risk. But great achievements also come from the hands of seemingly ordinary people with inordinate sets of Attributes, perfectly matched to bookend the knowledge they have and skills they possess to chase a specific dream.

Each of us drives the taxi that chauffeurs around our Attributes from one life challenge to the next. When chasing after those challenges, we can drive fast or we can drive slow.

Every night at midnight our hourglass releases another grain of sand. So, with that in mind, drive as fast as you can without having a wreck.

Hop #7: _Trust your skill to "See the End & Work Backward."_

By learning to "See the End & Work Backward" we've discovered that building airtight strategic plans is nowhere near as overwhelmingly hopeless or difficult as we previously thought. We now realize that by focusing on our Destination Objective, we can zero in precisely on what we expect to achieve.

Working back from there, we ask ourselves what two things (our Empowerment Objectives) must happen in order for our end goal to be produced.

We then smartly define our critical few (and necessary) Action Step Objectives to finish the baseline perimeter of our strategic plan.

Solid as tempered steel after being reality-tested, we confidently begin step-by-step flawlessly executing our plan. When finished, it delivers us to the unlocked front door of our castle of achievement.

Moss Alert: Be careful here. Moss can *cover* this rock if you let it. You must have a crystal clear focus on exactly what you hope to achieve and, above all, your end-vision *must* be realistically attainable.

Your strategic plan must be airtight and it must pass the Reality Test from top to bottom and back again. You must also be smart enough to have that Reality Test performed by someone whose primary intention is ripping it apart and finding its flaws. You can't be timid with a Reality Test. A timid jump won't get you safely atop the rock. You've got to hand your plan over and trust the quality of your work.

If not – if you *don't* pass it off to an outside resource – you'll be too myopic to critique your own strategy with the fresh, unbiased and challenging perspective it demands. Chances are you will miss something or, at the very least, blow the opportunity to do something within the plan better, faster, easier or more effectively.

Even when you've done everything right, bad timing can unfairly shove you off the rock anyway.

Strategic plan creation and flawless execution can reap great rewards. But if you fall off this rock before finishing the execution phase – *don't panic.* Keep climbing back out of the water and onto the rock. Persevere. If you've got a good plan, don't cheat yourself out of success because some of its execution is difficult. Stay the course.

Perched atop this rock and its vantage point, in the near distance you can see the PLT. You can even see the hammock with your name on it strung peacefully between the two palm trees.

There's only one more rock to hop on before broad-jumping firmly onto Life on the PLT.

Final Hop #8: *Never forget that "LIFE" is a 4-letter word.*

There's only one rock left between us and the PLT shoreline and in its stone face are carved three of Mortality's most ominous initials: "**S. E. E.**" *(for Significant Emotional Events).*

Significant Emotional Events are like pressure: They can make diamonds. But they can burst pipes, too.

We fully realize these emotional typhoons will show up unannounced from time-to-time. When they do, we've got to seek shelter until they pass. That's easier to say than do since the typhoons usually enter one ear en route to a dizzying eventual exit through the other. Sometimes the darn things even stall in mid-brain and seem in no particular hurry to leave.

Moss Alert: Most negative Significant Emotional Events are uncontrollable. Moss drips from this rock because we tend to treat *all* negative Significant Emotional Events as if they were intentionally sent to ruin our lives.

Conversely, many positive ones are *very much* controllable. Rarely do we take the time to Cherish and let linger the greatness of feeling and emotion that escorts life-enriching Significant Emotional Events directly through our heart and into the etching permanence of our soul.

We tend to dwell too much on sad memories we can't control (or change) and not dwell long enough on the magic of life's greatest moments.

How you handle stepping on the slippery moss – whether you skateboard it to safety or fly off into the water – is a test of maturity, balance and poise under fire. Significant Emotional Events produce adrenaline of great power and fury, often in set after set of relentless, pounding waves.

Sometimes these things will crush the will of a vulnerable soul. Other times they'll bring resolve and renewed energy to someone determined to persevere.

Managing these things – the Significant Emotional Events of your lifetime – is the last major test before hopping off to live a Life on the Pro Leisure Tour.

Now, for the book's final word, we'll defer to a tiny little man whose tremendous and perpetual worldwide fame blossomed from the unlikely fact that few of his admirers ever heard him speak.

The Final Word

A Tip of the Derby from "The Little Tramp"

The world teaches us that people are people everywhere and that talent, desire, ambition and work ethic know no cultural or geographic boundaries. Greatness is colorblind. So are kindness, passion, compassion, and motivation.

Mark Twain was perfectly right when he said, "People are all alike, on the inside." The magic of living and learning is fueled by collaborative diversity and life on the PLT reflects that.

PLT'ers don't have to look very far to realize how fortunate their lives have been. Travel around the world will teach that, but so will cursory trips around the valleys of every community.

Around 11% of today's Americans, some 32.3 million people, live below the family-of-four poverty level – a mere $17,029 in income per year. None of us, therefore, has to look much beyond our own neighborhood to find others to help teach how to climb the ladder of life's achievement. The attitude to proactively help others is a prevailing characteristic of everyone on the PLT.

An old baseball player best described how you could measure one person's singular meaning to society. "A man's life means nothing," he said, "except for the impact it has on others."

That was Jackie Robinson.

All Jackie ever wanted in life was a chance. A chance to compete. A chance to succeed or fail after he'd earned the right to find out which it would be.

And when Jackie got his chance, and had enough people believing in him to counteract those who didn't, Jackie succeeded. In doing so, he made the nation a better place for just about all of us.

Jackie's struggles as the first black man in Major League Baseball would've broken many a man less resolute. Throughout his protracted and often ugly battle for acceptance, Jackie always took the high road.

Jackie's impact on the PLT is pronounced. The PLT is a high road society comprised of people who want to help make a positive difference at home, in the office and in the community.

High road behaviors are an integral part of Pro Leisure Tour living for a simple reason: They add up. Beaches are made of grains of sand; ski resorts from snowflakes. Success is created the same way. Success – personal *and* professional – is the end result of a compiled series of effective behaviors.

PLT'ers are well aware that the only things in life they *can* control are their own thoughts, behaviors, and actions. But what PLT'ers *can* control, they *will* control. They focus on the facts – the truth – and inside their Worry Circles are allowed only those controllable problems that deserve to be there.

Many folks on the PLT chant this four-line ditty whenever the Worry Circle gremlins tie on their track shoes and start chasing them:

The Worry Song

"I get up and worry all day –
Then I go to bed.
One of these days if I don't quit worryin'
I'm-a-gonna wake up dead."

It's short. And it's sweet. But it's right to the point. PLT'ers *manage* what they worry about so <u>it</u> will never manage *them*.

How PLT'ers Deal with Situational Frustration

In my travels and training sessions, I've also seen an *army* of frustration out there that simply doesn't exist on the Pro Leisure Tour. Much of it seems to stem from three key things:

1. *The inability to manage worry and stress.*

2. *A personal lack of fulfilling and rewarding pursuits.*

3. *Poor time management and utilization.*

Learning to manage the Worry Circle (and we now know *how)* addresses the first common cause of frustration.

And number two – the lack of personal fulfillment – we can eliminate or at the very least, minimize. We know that a job is what we do to pay the bills. More importantly, we know that life is how we apply the money. As importantly, we know there are basically only three ways – not counting a windfall – for each of us to get rich:

a) *Accumulate wealth.* If you amass your material wealth by putting its pursuit above all else, you'll cheat yourself out of a whole lot of living. And worse, usually you'll be rich only when you waste the time to stop and count your money.

b) *Do good things for others.* The second point – being good to others – lets you be rich as you create that goodness for others, plus lets you be rich all over again whenever you sit back and reflect on what you've done. Internal richness is recession-proof. A life of goodness compounds memories, regardless of the state of the economy.

c) *Blend the two and meet in the middle.* The third wealth option – a blend of the first two – is especially rewarding when you invest your working time in something you love *and* it enables you to pursue a life that includes touching the lives of others.

Without that passion for what you do, the money you receive is merely that – a financial stipend for life hours spent – and not a rich payback for life hours rewardingly invested.

Personal Fulfillment

Internal contentment on the PLT blossoms from the conscious decisions you make concerning how you follow the decisions you've made (and written down) concerning who you truly want to be in life.

This deals with fulfilling the personal contract you made with yourself when you crafted your Daily Dozen. Every day for the rest of your life you'll make decisions relevant to work, home and community that are directly related to your ideals.

Simply taking absolute *ownership* of these decisions lowers life's directional rudder into the water off the transom of your personal sailboat. Once that rudder's in the water, *you* can now control your future direction regardless of the way the winds choose to blow.

When you weave your actions and activities through your core values and passions, you can't *help* but live a thoroughly enriched life. The emptiness comes when these things simply do not intersect. When your activities do not wrap around and braid your values or interests, everything in life is separately siloed. There's no interactive synergy between any of the things you do. Avoid that.

PLT'ers won't live that way. The fluid cohesion of fulfilling events requires that they stay true to their values while doing things they have a passion for. *They realize that contentment is self-created.* It is not randomly sprinkled from the heavens.

By understanding work's role in your life and how much of that life your chosen occupation truly consumes, you can then strive to maximize the value of every personal day your future brings. By never forgetting that time cannot be bought or sold, the true and absolute value of every grain of remaining sand in the top half of your life's hourglass becomes far more precious than most people ever realize.

Choosing to cherish, invest, spend, or waste our time are decisions that we, alone, control. On the PLT, very little time is ever wasted. PLT'ers cherish and invest greater portions of time than others. They are very well aware of its supreme value in living a fulfilling life.

By doing so, they also wipe off the third of those three common frustrations that so many countless others bounce and drag around like tin cans behind a newlywed's bumper. Poor time management and utilization simply are not found in PLT lifestyles.

The PLT can be an amazing springboard to future accomplishment. The deep-rooted gallery of historical achievement demonstrates how otherwise ordinary people applied their personalized set of KSA's to achieve extraordinary things in pursuits they had a unyielding passion for. Here are a few examples:

♦ **Leo Tolstoy flunked out of college.**

But Tolstoy's passion was writing, not studying. Tolstoy persevered and became one of the greatest writers in Russian history, chronicling life in socialist Russia during the last half of the 19th century.

♦ **Einstein didn't learn to speak until after he turned four.**

It took three *more* years, until the age of seven, before young Albert finally learned to read. A four-year-old kid who can't speak and a seven-year-old kid who can't read would be considered by many to be prime candidates for eventual enshrinement in the Survivor Hall of Fame.

But Einstein's family and instructors never thought so. After that tortoise-like academic beginning and buoyed by the confidence his surrounding circle of adult mentors, Albert sort of picked up the pace a little bit and became one of the greatest Thrivers in the modern history of the planet.

♦ **The brilliant music composer Josef Haydn finally gave up in frustration after trying unsuccessfully to teach a young student.**

269

Haydn's pupil seemed very slow, had no apparent talent and nothing going for him other than an unfailing love of music.

Who was the pupil? Beethoven. What Beethoven had – way before talent – was a boundless passion for some-thing he desperately wanted to learn: Music.

It was Beethoven's *passion* that stoked the eternal flame of his eventual relentless genius. Beethoven's developing Knowledge and Skills lagged way behind his Attributes.

♦ **And if you're over 35 and harbor political aspirations, keep one other guy in mind, too.**

Poet Carl Sandburg said this fellow was made out of "velvet and steel." The fellow lost nine elections, his business went under, he buried a girlfriend, and a year later had a nervous breakdown.

This guy had a Worry Circle the circumference of the equator, plus endured a series of Significant Emotional Events that would fill a fat hardbound textbook.

But the man forged on, often buried in the depths of his loneliness, and battled through the pain. He had a truly unbreakable spirit.

Know whom Sandburg was talking about? Give yourself 10 points if you answered "Abraham Lincoln." Give yourself 10 bonus points if you knew that, despite his life's assembly line of relentless personal and professional setbacks, Lincoln pushed forward and achieved his legendary life's work despite a sandtimer holding just 56 years worth of granules.

Keep Plugging

These greats all left footprints because they all kept plugging. And that's what people on the PLT do: They keep plugging. Busy people – achievers – have no finish lines. They keep making things happen until their very last grain of sand drops gently through the top of life's hourglass to crown the peak of the pile on the bottom.

What the Future Holds: *The Impact of Trends in Education & Diversity*

The U.S. population is showing dramatic demographic growth among Asians and Latins. As these cultural representations continue to expand throughout all segments of education, science and industry, so too will the number of diverse Thrivers who emerge and contribute as leaders through-out the entirety of the 21st century.

Women of all cultures will continue to increase their power and influence.

Nearly 100 years ago, Marie Curie became the first female Nobel Prize winner. Shortly thereafter, she became the first woman to win two of them in different disciplines. A Polish woman, Mme. Curie won first for her Physics research at the age of 36. Eight years later, in 1911, she won a second Nobel Prize for Chemistry.

Her work eventually killed her. *Why* she chose the work she did is revealing.

"You cannot hope to build a better world without improving the individuals," Mme. Curie said. "To that end, each of us must work for our own improvement and, at the same time, share a general responsibility for all humanity, our particular duty being to aid those to whom we think we can be most useful."

Mme. Curie specialized in radioactivity research. When World War I broke out, she developed the portable X-ray machine to help save the wounded. She also trained 150 female attendants how to properly use the devices. Her passion forever changed world medicine and paved the way for the acceptance of women scientists around the world.

In many ways, her message was identical to Jackie Robinson's a half-century later.

Marie Curie's greatness came partly from a shouldered belief that it was her duty – her calling – to help others if she could. That belief fueled her passion and research. In the end, her life's work

271

forced her to pay the ultimate price. She died in 1934 from leukemia, most likely brought on by prolonged radiation exposure.

Since her glass-ceiling-shattering work, 28 other women have followed Mme. Curie's lead. Women have now won the Nobel Prize in every category except Economics, which wasn't established until 1968. Before long, a woman will win that one, too.

The reason why is simple: There's a dramatic global escalation of high-performing, culturally diverse Thrivers entering the world stage from all corners of the globe.

Domestically, more women than men are seeking higher education and post-graduate degrees. Key fields of advancement, including medicine, show a dramatic acceleration of women as the formerly top-heavy male work demographic ages toward retirement.

Women now outnumber men at nearly all levels of higher education. In the three areas they don't – Doctoral degrees, Medical degrees, and Law degrees – women are quickly and dramatically narrowing the diploma gap. The chart on the next page summarizes current American college trends.

Breakdown, by Sex, of College Degree Recipients

College Degree:	Female Grads	Male Grads
College Associate of Arts	56.3%	43.7%
Bachelor Degrees	60.0%	40.0%
Masters Degrees	57.7%	42.3%
Doctoral Degrees *	40.0% *	60.0%
Medical Degrees **	41.0%**	59.0%
Law Degrees ***	44.0%***	56.0%

(all figures from The World Almanac, 2001 Edition)

Trend Summary in Advanced Degrees:

* -- Doctoral Degrees: Women grads have ***increased*** from 14% to 40% since the early 1970s.

* * -- Medical Degrees: Women grads have ***increased*** from 8% to 41% since the early 1970s.

* * * -- Law Degrees: Women grads have ***increased*** from 5% to 44% since the early 1970s.)

The Income Gap Will Continue to Narrow

Women continue to be paid, on-average, less than men with commensurate credentials. But the gap is narrowing. Proportionately, at the start of the new millennium, women were being paid roughly 73.2% of what men earn, up significantly from 58.8% in 1975. At that rate, by 2041 the gap will be closed and women will finally reach financial parity.

But that gap closure – payment parity – *should* arrive much sooner. As more and more advanced degree women enter the marketplace than men, the increased demand for their services will force those salary figures to accelerate upward.

Plus, the men's traditional earning power from their generations-ago head start will dissipate. In traditionally male-oriented industries like medicine and law, many of those older males will retire and women will assume these responsibilities.

Increasingly, women will earn and assume more leadership positions and be paid accordingly. They, in turn, will open the door to even more quality opportunities for additional female Thrivers.

The Magic Formula

Throughout the book we've talked about women and men who've used their knowledge, skills and special sets of attributes to follow their passions. Their achievements have changed the landscape around them.

There is no magic success "formula." Once you set your mind to it, there are a million ways to succeed – but very few depend on blind luck or divine intervention.

What all this means, of course, is that as we look to the immediate future, personal achievement will know no boundaries.

Everything starts with the vision and expectations you hold for yourself. Then, by marrying the right knowledge, skills and attributes to your challenge at-hand, you will earn, experience, and deserve success.

Many barriers to success are temporary and can methodically be worked around. After all, every explorer bumps his or her head on a tree. Few do it twice on the same limb, but every single one conks their curious noggin from time-to-time.

Some explorers break new ground by extensively planning their travels before shoving off. Others are wanderers and learn as they go. The magic comes in the learned perseverance they demonstrate over time.

The late rock superstar John Lennon was the voice of his generation and Lennon steadfastly insisted on living in the present. He never looked over his shoulder.

Lennon lived by the day, for the day. In that regard, he was very much like Oprah. What Lennon saw surrounding him was dramatically different, but his all-encompassing focus on the present rather than the past or future is very similar to Oprah's outlook on life. Her passion is cherishing today more than planning travels down the road. Oprah lives *in* the moment, *for* the moment.

"Because it's there."

Both George Mallory and Sir Edmund Hillary have been credited with that response, when each was asked why he decided to climb Mt. Everest. I'm not sure who said it first, but I *do* know that Hillary's the only one who made it back down to hear the question repeated. Hillary was a quiet, unassuming New Zealand beekeeper, so my guess is they're Mallory's words. Mallory died on the mountain and now – decades later – his prone frozen body remains face down on the mountaintop near Everest's peak.

Recently a blind man, Colorado's Erik Weihenmayer, reached Everest's summit at the age of 32 – a full 19 years after losing his sight to a degenerative eye disease. Erik knew not his limitations. Just because no blind man had climbed Everest before didn't mean he couldn't at least try.

Weihenmayer reached the top right behind 64-year-old Sherman Bull, who became the oldest man to summit the 29,035-foot peak. The day before, a Russian climber died trying. The Russian was the fourth fatality of the climbing season.

Weihenmayer said he was plagued by self-doubt hundreds of times every day, but just kept putting one struggling foot in front of the other. For direction, he followed the sound of a bell secured to the jacket of the climber in front of him.

A Tibetan proverb endlessly replaying between his ears helped Erik finally reach the top. Over and over he kept repeating, "The nature of the mind is like water. If you don't stir it, it will remain clear." Erik couldn't control the miserable legions of uncontrollables swirling all around him, but he *could control* his will to stubbornly follow the faint ringing of the bell above him.

When Weihenmayer finally summited, he was 20 pounds lighter than when he first began his climb. He stayed at the top of the world for 10 minutes. Fellow climbers described the sights and scenery to him.

"I don't harp on the things that I can't do or can't experience," he said later. "I try to soak up as much as I can with the senses I have."

Achievements like the seemingly impossible one Weihenmayer pulled off don't just happen. They take dreams, vision, planning, commitment, persistence and execution. Erik also channeled his energy toward what he could control and refused to get lost in the distractive smoke-bombs of the uncontrollable.

The more efficiently you can incorporate those critical skills into your life and business pursuits, the more success you'll experience. I've written this book specifically to help people better understand not just what to do but, more importantly, to do those things with maximum straight-line efficiency using skills that are interchangeable throughout all facets of living.

"The Little Champ" Shares His Secret

In closing, there's one final success factor you must never forget. And for it, I'll defer to a tiny little man who's been gone for quite some time now but whose life-sized statue on the shores of Lake Geneva welcomes you to the scenic lakefront hamlet of Vevey, Switzerland.

In 1931 an interviewer looked at the great comedy legend Charlie Chaplin calmly seated before him and asked, quite bluntly, how he did it. What *was* the secret to Chaplin's success? How did he keep coming up with the seemingly endless procession of great new ideas that made the entire world laugh time after time after time?

276

Chaplin's answer is just as true now as it was nearly 70 years ago when he gently gave his reply.

After hearing the question, Chaplin sat back, thought for a moment, then slowly smiled. He paused, then leaned forward toward the man who asked the question.

In a loud whisper, Chaplin revealed the source of the magic. "You have to believe in yourself," he said. *"That's* the secret."

Happy with his answer, Chaplin smiled, folded his arms in satisfied triumph and leaned back again in his chair.

And because Chaplin followed his own advice, he made the world a little better place.

The future is out there. And it's yours. Commit yourself to remember Chaplin's special secret and promise, above all, to always believe in yourself. Live life. Love the journey. And have lots of fun along the way.

Best of luck to you always – with every dream you choose to reach.

Contact the Author:

For questions, comments and observations, feel free to contact the author directly, either electronically or in writing.

E-mail: theo@richwithoutmoney.com

Mailing address:

Ted Simendinger
Pro Leisure Tour, Inc.
P.O. Box 4434
Greenwood Village, CO 80111-4434